# MASTERING DOG TRAINING:

## The Ultimate Puppy Guide for Kids, Teens, and Adults

Successfully Navigating the Exciting and Challenging First Year of Dog Training with Your Puppy

From the Pets Series

By Max Biscuit

# COPYRIGHT & DISCLAIMER



Disclaimer

The author and publisher of this book have made every effort to ensure the accuracy and completeness of the information contained herein. However, dog training practices, safety measures, and the behaviours and characteristics of individual dogs can vary widely. Therefore, the author, publisher, and anyone associated with this book cannot be held responsible for any accident, injury, or damage caused to any person or property, whether physical or mental, as a result of attempting to implement or use the information presented in this book.

Training a dog should always be undertaken with the supervision and assistance of an adult and, where necessary, professional advice should be sought before proceeding with the activities suggested in this book. It is the reader's responsibility to ensure their own safety and that of their dog when attempting any training methods or games outlined in this book.

Always consult with a professional dog trainer or veterinarian if you have questions or concerns about your dog's behaviour or health. This book describes a variety of training methods and techniques, all of which depend on the individual dog and its owner. The author and publisher are not responsible for any negative or harmful results obtained through the application of the methods and advice found in this book.

# CONTENTS

# NOTE TO PARENTS / ADULTS

Dear Adults,

We're thrilled that you've picked up "*Mastering Dog Training: The Ultimate Puppy Guide for Kids, Teens, and Adults.*" Thank you!

If you're reading this, it's likely because you and your family have decided to embark on the **extraordinary journey** of welcoming a new puppy into your home.

This is more than just a book; it's a guide to **building a bond with your new family member** that will last a lifetime. Your teenager **or you as an adult** has taken a significant step by deciding to be an active participant in this process.

Whether you already have a new furry friend at home or are just beginning to consider adopting one, this guide **is here to help** you through every step of the journey.

**Our previous book**, "*Puppy Training 101: A Practical Guide for Young Dog Owners,*" catered to **younger dog owners**, teaching them the basic skills of puppy training. This book, on the other hand, is designed with the **growing maturity of your children and adults in mind**. It offers more complex training, understanding canine psychology, and real-world scenarios that **adults and teens** can relate to.

As we navigate through the challenges and joys of the first year with a new puppy, **remember** that these experiences are invaluable for the development of your child. These experiences teach **responsibility, compassion, patience, and empathy**, which are crucial life skills.

One essential point to **remember** throughout this process is that there's no such thing as perfection.

Training a puppy comes with its ups and downs, and sometimes, it might feel like two steps forward, one step back. **Encourage your child and yourself** when the progress seems slow, and **celebrate the victories**, no matter how small they might seem.

Training a puppy is **as much about learning as it is about teaching**.

Throughout this journey, your family **will learn** more about communication, understanding, and mutual respect. These lessons are as beneficial for us humans as they are for our canine companions.

Your role as a parent is critical in this journey. **Be there to support and guide your child**, but allow them to take the lead in training and nurturing their puppy. Let them make mistakes and learn from them. It's all part of the process.

**For those adults** embarking on this journey without kids, **remember** that patience and consistency are key. Whether you're a first-time dog owner **or revisiting the experience**, every dog is **unique** and offers a fresh opportunity to forge a lasting bond. Embrace every moment, the **challenges and the joys alike**, knowing that the time and effort you invest will result in a **rewarding partnership**. This guide is here **to support you** every step of the way, ensuring that both you and your furry companion thrive together.

Please use this book as a tool, a companion, and a **source of inspiration** throughout your puppy training journey.

We wish you and your family countless happy moments, belly rubs, tail wags, and a **friendship** that only grows stronger over time.

Happy Training,

Paws and puppy licks,

Your Puppy Training Guide

Max Biscuit

https://www.maxbiscuit.com

**Unlock** a world of pet care wisdom! Scan to explore Max Biscuit's top book picks, expert tips, and grab your **FREE subscription** to our exclusive newsletter.

*Photo by Jametlene Reskp on Unsplash*

# WELCOME TO YOUR TRAINING JOURNEY - READY, SET, WOOF!

**Hello there, puppy parents and dog devotees!**

Welcome to the start of a wonderful adventure—raising a puppy! Your journey as a puppy parent is about to get more exciting, more rewarding, and (let's be honest) a bit more challenging. But don't worry, we're here to guide you through the rollercoaster ride of puppyhood with *"Mastering Dog Training: The Ultimate Puppy Guide for Kids, Teens, and Adults"*.

**The first year** of a puppy's life **is an important period**, filled with rapid growth, abundant energy, and plenty of adorable moments. It's also a time of **significant learning for both you and your furry friend**. Just like children, puppies are curious, love to explore, and are quick to pick up new behaviours—both good and bad.

**But don't fret!** That's where this guide comes in.

This book is designed to be your **go-to resource** throughout your first year with your puppy. We've broken down the complex world of **puppy training into fun, easy-to-understand lessons**. With our help, you'll learn **how to navigate** everything from housebreaking plus crate training, and basic obedience, to socializing, and even handling the dreaded "puppy teething".

Plus, **each lesson** is packed with pro tips, interesting puppy facts, and plenty of humor to keep you entertained. Because we believe that **training should be fun**, not a chore!

**Remember**, raising a puppy isn't just about molding them into well-behaved adult dogs. It's about **building a strong bond of trust, understanding, and love**.

So, **let's make this first year count!**

Are you ready to embark on the most rewarding journey of your life?

Let's dive in, **paw-first**, into the captivating world of puppy training.

**Happy training, puppy parents!**

*Photo by **Elena Mozhvilo** on Unsplash*

# PUPPY BASICS

## Hey there, future puppy parents!

**Before we jump** into the delightful chaos of puppy training, let's make sure we understand some puppy basics. After all, understanding your new furry friend is the **key to successful training** and a harmonious relationship.

In our previous guide, *"Puppy Training 101: A Practical Guide for Young Dog Owners"*, we touched on various aspects of dog training. This time, we're dialing it back a bit and **starting from the beginning: puppyhood**. And just like humans, **every puppy is unique**, with its own personality, quirks, and learning pace.

So, let's dive into the **enchanting world of puppies!**

## Age Matters

Puppies are typically ready to leave their mother and go to their new homes **at about 8 weeks old**. This age is crucial because it's the start of the puppy's socialization period.

This time is essential for puppies to learn how to **interact with the world** around them.

## Understanding Puppy Development Stages

Puppies go through **various stages** as they grow. These stages are generally broken down as follows:

- Neonatal period (0-2 weeks)
- Transitional period (2-4 weeks)
- Socialization period (4-12 weeks)
- Juvenile period (3-6 months)
- Adolescence (6-18 months)

**Understanding** these stages will give you insight into your puppy's behavior and developmental needs at different times.

## Puppy Health

Your puppy's health is a **top priority**. Regular vet check-ups combined with **a balanced diet, and plenty of exercise** are crucial. Also, make sure your puppy gets all the necessary vaccinations and treatments for parasites.

## The Power of Play

Never underestimate the power of play! It's not just about fun (although, it's a HUGE part), it's also an **important learning tool**.

Puppies learn about their world, social norms, and even bite inhibition **through play**. Plus, playtime is a great way to bond with your puppy and **drain** some of that boundless energy.

## Patience is Key

Finally, **remember that patience is key** in all aspects of puppy raising.

Mistakes and accidents **will happen**—it's part of the process. **Your calm**, consistent responses will help your puppy learn.

And there you have it!

A brief overview of some puppy basics. **Keep these in mind** as we embark on this puppy-raising adventure together.

# Now, **let's fetch some knowledge about puppy training!**

*Photo by **Hendo Wang** on Unsplash*

# PREPARING FOR PUPPY ARRIVAL

**Oh, the excitement of a new puppy coming home!**

It's like the anticipation of a new school year, mixed with the thrill of embarking on a grand adventure, with a dash of the joy of making a new best friend.

But let's make sure we are ready for this ball of energy, joy, and fluff that is about to **enter your life!**

Remember, we can not **stressed enough the importance of preparation**. It's no different when it comes to bringing a puppy home.

**Being well-prepared** not only makes the **transition smoother** for your new furry friend but also for everyone else in your household.

So, what does preparing for a puppy entail?

## Puppy-proofing Your Home

Think of this as **similar to baby-proofing**, but for a fast-growing, curious pup who loves to explore with its mouth.

Make sure cleaning supplies, medications, and other potentially harmful substances are out of reach. **Secure loose electrical cords**, keep shoes and other chewable items away, and make sure your yard is escape-proof.

Also, be prepared for some potential damage. **Remember, they are still learning!**

## Choosing the Right Gear

It's **like getting your school supplies** before the term starts. A **comfortable** collar and leash, an ID tag, food and water bowls, a crate (if you choose to crate train), puppy food, a bed, and lots of toys (for chewing and playing) **are some of the essentials**.

## Setting Up a Puppy Zone

Having a **designated space** for your puppy helps them **feel secure** and aids in training. This area should have their bed, some toys, and water available.

## Planning for Vet Visits

**Find a vet you trust.** Your puppy will **need a check-up soon after adoption** and will need regular vaccinations and treatments for parasites.

## Planning the Nutrition

Just like you wouldn't fuel a sports car with low-grade fuel, you wouldn't want to feed your growing puppy sub-par food. Check with your vet for **recommendations based on your puppy's** breed, size, and health.

## Toilet Training Strategy

**Decide on your strategy** ahead of time. Are you going to paper train first? Or go straight to outdoor training? Where will the designated bathroom spot be?

## Basic Command Training

Think about the first few commands you want to teach your

puppy. **Usually**, "sit", "stay", "come", and "no" are good places to start.

## Creating a Routine

**Puppies, like kids**, do well with a routine. Think about feeding times, toilet breaks, playtimes, training times, and quiet times. **Don't worry, we'll delve more into creating a successful routine later in the book**!

Bringing home a new puppy is an **exciting time** full of joy, laughter, and a few challenges.

**Remember**, every new experience for your puppy **is a training opportunity** and a chance to **strengthen your bond**. Enjoy the journey and embrace the mess.

And hey, isn't that what all the best adventures are made of?

# BASIC TRAINING

Hey there, dear readers! Welcome to the "Basic Training" section of our **ultimate** puppy guide.

After going through the excitement of preparing for your new pup in the previous chapter, we're now getting into the **nitty-gritty**.

It's time to roll up our sleeves and get into some **doggy education!**

**Remember**, this is not about transforming your cute little furball into a disciplined soldier. Oh no!

We're just **teaching them** the rules of our human world **so they can navigate** it with ease, joy, and safety. And if you've read our previous book, "*Puppy Training 101: A Practical Guide for Young Dog Owners*", you'll be familiar with some of the teaching methods we're going to use.

## The Essentials

What are the basics that every puppy should learn?

You're probably thinking of commands like 'sit', 'stay', and 'come'. And you're right! But **basic training isn't just about**

**teaching commands**. It's about creating a **communication channel** between you and your puppy. It's about teaching them **how to behave** in our human world and how to **interact** with different beings and objects.

**But don't worry!**

You won't need to become a professional dog trainer overnight. In this chapter, we'll break down these essential skills **into bite-sized lessons**. We'll take you through step-by-step, ensuring that you and your new buddy can tackle each new learning experience **with confidence**.

## Understanding Your Puppy

Before we dive into the practical side of training, let's talk about understanding your puppy.

Your puppy is not just a furry little creature, but **a sentient being with thoughts, feelings, and instincts**. They have their own ways of **understanding and interacting** with the world. By understanding these, you'll be able to communicate and train your puppy **more effectively.**

This might sound complicated, **but don't worry!**

As we go through the various elements of training, we'll also be learning about dog **behaviour and psychology.** This way, you'll not only know what to do but understand why you're doing it. And who knows, you might even end up being the local dog whisperer in your neighbourhood!

## Patience and Consistency

Training your puppy needs a lot of **patience and consistency**. We all know how tempting it is to let your adorable pup get away with naughty behaviour. But **remember**, **consistency is key** to successful training.

**We're building habits here**, and habits take time and repetition to form.

But don't fret.

Even if some days seem challenging, **remember that every small step you take is an investment in your future relationship with your dog**. Plus, there's always a solution to every challenge, and that's where this guide comes in.

In the upcoming sections, we'll be diving into specifics. We'll cover everything from potty training and leash walking to teaching basic commands and curtailing bad habits.

**We're here to guide you** through every step of this incredible journey.

So, buckle up and **get ready for some doggy education**. This is going to be a tail-wagging adventure!

*Photo by **Joe Caione** on Unsplash*

# LESSON 1: UNDERSTANDING DOG BEHAVIOR AND COMMUNICATION

**Reason**: You might be thinking, "Why is this lesson even important? I want to teach my puppy to sit and stay, not have a heart-to-heart conversation!"

But here's the thing: **understanding** your puppy's behaviour and **communication is the foundation of all the training** that will happen.

When you know **how your puppy communicates**, you can understand what they're feeling and how they're likely to react in different situations. It's like learning a **new language**. Once you understand it, you'll have a **better relationship** with your furry friend!

**Goal**: The goal of this lesson is to **learn the basics of dog communication and behaviour**. By the end of it, you'll have a better understanding of how dogs "speak" through their body language, sounds, and actions.

**Hint:** Just like how we use different tones of voice to express ourselves, dogs use **different types** of barks, whines, and growls. So, **pay attention** to the sounds your dog makes in different situations.

**Step-by-Step**

## Watch your puppy's body language

Dogs communicate very much through their body language. **Watch** how your puppy behaves in different situations. Do they wag their tail when they're happy? Do their ears go back when they're scared? Do they lower their body when they're feeling threatened? These are all **clues** about what your puppy is feeling.

## Listen to the sounds your puppy makes

Dogs make a variety of sounds - barks, whines, howls, growls. These sounds **can mean different things** depending on the situation. A high-pitched bark might mean your dog is excited, while a low growl could mean they're feeling threatened.

## Notice your puppy's behavior around people and other animals

How your puppy behaves around others can **give you a lot of information**. Are they excited and friendly, or are they more reserved and cautious? This can help you **understand** your puppy's temperament and socialization needs.

## Observe your puppy's behavior in different environments

Take your puppy to different places - the park, the vet, a busy street. Notice how they react in these environments. This can tell you about their **comfort levels and fears**.

## Take notes

It can be helpful to jot down what you notice about **your puppy's behavior**. This can help you **track any changes** and could be useful information for your vet or a professional dog trainer.

By observing and understanding your puppy's behaviour and communication, you're setting a **strong foundation** for the rest of your training sessions.

**Remember**, every dog is unique. So, what works for one dog might not work for another. Keep an open mind, and **remember - patience is key!**

Stay tuned for the next lesson where we'll be diving into the wonderful world of puppy socialization.

**Happy training!**

*Photo by **Taylor Sondgeroth** on Unsplash*

# LESSON 2: SOCIALIZATION

**Reason**: Have you ever met **a dog that's scared of everything**, from the vacuum cleaner to the neighbour's cat? Or a dog that barks at every other dog on the street? This is often because they **weren't properly socialized as a puppy**.

Socialization is a **crucial part** of your puppy's development. It helps them become **confident**, well-adjusted dogs who know how to behave around people, animals, and in different environments.

**Goal**: The goal of this lesson is to **introduce your puppy** to as many **new experiences** as possible in a controlled and safe manner. By the end of this lesson, your puppy should be comfortable around people of different ages, sizes, and ethnicities, and around other animals, noises, and environments.

**Hint**: The prime socialization period for puppies is between **3 to 12 weeks old**. It's when they're most open to new experiences. So, **the sooner you can start, the better!**

**Step-by-Step**

### Introduce your puppy to different people

Invite friends and family over to meet your puppy. Make sure **they're gentle and calm around your puppy**. Give your friends treats to give to your puppy. This helps your puppy associate new **people with good things**.

### Introduce your puppy to different environments

Take your puppy to different places – the park, a pet-friendly café, a busy street, the beach. Let them experience **different sights, smells, and sounds**. Always keep your puppy **on a leash for safety**.

### Introduce your puppy to different noises

Expose your puppy to different sounds – the vacuum cleaner, the washing machine, the sound of cars, the sound of children playing. Start with low volumes and **gradually** increase the volume as your puppy gets comfortable.

### Introduce your puppy to other animals

If you have friends or neighbours with vaccinated and friendly pets, arrange a playdate. **Make sure the other animal is okay with puppies** and that the **interaction is supervised**.

### Join a puppy socialization class

Many vet clinics and pet stores offer **puppy socialization classes**. These classes are an excellent way for your puppy to meet other puppies and learn how to **interact appropriately**.

**Remember**, socialization **should be a positive experience** for your puppy.

**Never force** your puppy into a situation they're uncomfortable with. If they're scared, back off and try again later.

It's all about **baby steps**.

And **as always**, for a broader understanding of dog behaviours and training tips.

Happy training!

Why don't dogs make good dancers?

Because they have two left feet!

**Important**, socializing your puppy may feel like a dance where you both are stepping on each other's toes at first. But with time and practice, you both will learn the rhythm!

Keep dancing, and keep laughing!

*For much more details go directly to the "Socialization and Habituation" section below.*

# LESSON 3: NAME RECOGNITION

**Reason**: One of the first steps in your puppy training adventure is teaching your furry friend to respond to their name. **A dog's name is a crucial command**, as it serves as the foundation for future training and commands.

It helps get **your dog's attention** and prepares them to respond to whatever you ask next. **It's also a safety measure**. If your dog ever escapes or gets loose, you'll need them to respond to their name to get them back safely.

**Goal**: By the end of this lesson, your goal should be that your puppy **consistently and reliably** responds to their name, **no matter what kind of distractions** may be around them.

The puppy should stop what they're doing and give you their full attention when they hear their name. This is crucial for the next steps in training, where more complex commands will be introduced.

**Hint**: Choose a name **that is clear, concise, and distinct**. Avoid names that sound similar to commands you'll be teaching later on (like "sit" and "Kit"). Also, ensure all family members consistently **use the same name**. If you have a long or fancy registered name for your dog, consider a shorter everyday nickname that's easy for your puppy to recognize.

**Step-by-Step**

## Choose the Right Environment

Start in a quiet, **distraction-free environment**. Your living room or backyard would be great.

## Get Their Attention

Get down on their level, so you are more interesting to them than the floor or the sky. Make sure you have **some treats handy**.

## Say Their Name

Look at your puppy and say their name in a clear, happy, enthusiastic voice. **Don't yell**, but don't whisper either. **Make it fun!**

## Reward Their Attention

**If they look at you or even glance in your direction**, give them a treat and lots of praise immediately. They need to **associate** their name with good things happening.

## Gradual Increase in Distraction

Once your puppy is reliably responding to their name in a quiet place, start practicing in **gradually** more distracting environments - the yard, during playtimes, when other family members are around, and so forth.

## Keep It Positive

Never use your puppy's name in anger or frustration. It should always be **associated with good things**.

**Remember**, patience is key.

Some puppies might get this in a day, while others might take a week or two. **Every puppy is different**. Keep practicing, **keep it positive**, and soon your puppy will be responding to their name like a champ!

In our previous book, *"Puppy Training 101: A Practical Guide for Young Dog Owners"*, we emphasized the importance of **patience, consistency, and positive reinforcement**. This remains just as true for our new canine companions.

**Happy training!**

Stay tuned for the next lesson, where we'll be diving into potty training – a crucial, albeit sometimes messy, part of puppy training.

*For much more details go directly to the "Name Recognition" section below.*

*Photo by **Daniël Maas** on Unsplash*

# LESSON 4: HOUSEBREAKING/ POTTY TRAINING

**Reason**: Housebreaking, or potty training, is a **fundamental part** of bringing a new puppy home.

This process teaches your puppy the right places (and the wrong places!) to relieve themselves. It's essential for maintaining a clean, healthy home environment and is a **critical first step** in your life with your new puppy.

**Goal**: By the end of this lesson, your goal should be that your puppy **consistently goes to the bathroom in the correct place**, whether that's outside in your backyard, on a walk, or on puppy pads if necessary.

**Hint: Remember**, puppies have small bladders and limited control. They'll need to go out often, including after meals, playtime, naps, and before bed. **Consistency and patience are key** in housebreaking.

The use of **rewards and positive reinforcement** will make this process faster and more efficient.

Just like we stressed in our previous book, **punishment does not help** in training and can actually set back progress.
**Step-by-Step**

### Establish a Routine

Puppies do best on a **regular schedule**. Take your puppy outside **frequently**—at least **every two hours**, and immediately after they wake up, during and after playtime, and after eating or drinking.

### Pick a Potty Spot

Choose a bathroom spot outside. While always using a leash take your puppy to that spot. While your puppy is doing his business **use a specific word or phrase** you will always use before they go to remind them what to do.

### Praise and Reward

Praise your puppy lavishly every time they eliminate outdoors. You can even give them a treat. But **remember** to **praise them immediately after** they've finished, not after they come back inside. **This step is vital**: praising your dog for going outdoors is the only way to teach **what's expected of them**.

### Limit Inside Freedom Until Fully Trained

A **common mistake** is giving a puppy **too much freedom too soon**. During the early stages of training, keep an eye on them and limit their unsupervised time indoors.

### Handle Accidents Calmly

**Accidents are a normal** part of house training your new puppy. When your puppy has an accident, clean it up **calmly and quietly. Don't punish your puppy** - this can actually make things worse.

### Use a Crate

When you can't watch your puppy closely, they should be in a crate or pen, or a small, puppy-proof room where accidents won't damage the flooring.

**Remember**, some puppies will learn this quickly while others may take more time.

**Don't worry,** every puppy learns at their own pace. **Be patient, persistent, and keep a positive attitude,** and your puppy will get there!

Soon, your puppy will be ringing a bell by the door or giving you a specific look when they need to go outside.

**Each small success** will bring such joy, showing you that all the patience and consistency was worth it.

Happy training!

Why don't puppies make good secret keepers?

Because they always spill the "poo-p"!

*For much more details go directly to the "Housebreaking/Potty Training" section below.*

*Photo by **Ayla Verschueren** on Unsplash*

# LESSON 5: CRATE TRAINING

**Reason**: A crate can be a safe and comfortable space for your puppy, a place they can call their own. **It's not a prison**; think of it more like **a cozy bedroom**.

Crate training can help with housebreaking, as dogs naturally avoid soiling their sleeping area. It can also help **prevent destructive behaviour** when you're not around to supervise.

**Goal**: The aim of crate training is to make your puppy **feel comfortable and secure** in their crate, willingly entering when it's time for them to sleep or when you need them to be safely contained.

Step-by-Step

## Choosing the Crate

First things first, choose a crate that's just large enough for your puppy to stand up, turn around, and lie down comfortably. **If it's too large**, your puppy might use one corner as a bathroom.

## Making it Comfortable

Add some cozy bedding and favourite toys. Making the crate **a pleasant place** encourages your puppy to spend time there.

## Introduction

Start by leaving the crate door open, letting your pup explore. If they don't seem interested, try tossing in **a few treats or a favourite toy**.

## Mealtime

Feed your puppy's meals in the crate with the door open to **create positive associations**.

## Closing the Door

**Once your puppy is comfortable**, try closing the door while they're eating or playing with a toy. Start with a few minutes and **gradually** increase the time as long as your puppy remains calm.

## Nighttime and Naptime

**Encourage** your pup to sleep in their crate at night and during nap times. This will also help with potty training since puppies usually don't soil their sleeping area.

## Leaving Home

Start using the crate when you leave the house **for short periods**. **Never make a big fuss** when you leave or return home, as this can cause anxiety.

**Remember**, crate training takes patience and consistency. **Never use the crate as a punishment**. Always create a **positive environment** for your puppy.

**Hint:** Some puppies might cry or whine the first few times they're in the crate. It's important not to let them out while they're making noise, or they'll learn that crying gets them out. **Instead**, wait for a **temporary interval of quiet** in the noise before letting them out.

This basic training is the first step towards **creating a strong bond and a harmonious living environment** with your new buddy.

Enjoy the process, **take your time**!

**Keep at it, be patient**, and soon enough, your puppy will be crate trained. It's a step-by-step process, but you and your puppy are taking those steps together!

Why did the dog sit in the shade?

Because he didn't want to become a hot dog!

*Photo by **Brady Wakely** on **Unsplash***

# LESSON 6: LEASH WALKING

**Reason**: Leash walking is a **crucial skill** for every dog to master. Not only does it ensure their safety during outdoor activities, but it also allows for controlled, calm, and enjoyable walks. **Your arm will thank you!**

**Goal**: The goal is to have your pup **walking nicely** on a leash without pulling or tugging. They should be able to walk at your pace and follow your direction changes.

**Hint**: Patience and consistency **are key**. Some puppies might get the hang of leash walking quite quickly, while others may need more time. **Remember**, every puppy is unique!

Step-by-Step

## Start Indoors

Begin leash training indoors or in a **low-distraction environment**. This will make it easier for your puppy to concentrate.

## Introduce the Leash

Let your puppy get used to the feeling of a leash. Attach the leash and **let them drag it** around (under your watchful eye, of course). **Reward them** for behaving calmly with the leash on.

## First Steps

With the leash in your hand, call your puppy's name and start walking. Use **a positive, encouraging voice** to get your puppy moving.

## Use Treats for Motivation

Keep some tasty treats in your hand. Hold your hand next to you at your hip level, where you'd like your pup to be while walking. As they follow the treat, **praise and reward** them.

## Teach a Cue for Walking Nicely

As your puppy starts to understand the concept of walking at your side, you can **introduce a cue word** like "heel" or "let's go."

## Correcting Course

If your puppy starts pulling on the leash, stop walking. **Don't yank on the leash**; instead, call their name and lure them back to your side with a treat. Once they're back at your side, **start walking again**.

## Gradual Progression

As your puppy gets more comfortable walking on a leash indoors, slowly start introducing them to the outdoors. **Start with short walks** and gradually increase the distance as your puppy gets better at leash walking.

**Remember**, just like with every new skill, **this is a process that takes time.**

There will be good days and some not-so-good days. Keep the training sessions **short, fun, and positive**.

**Your patience and consistency** will soon pay off with lovely, relaxed walks with your best buddy.

*Photo by **Berkay Gumustekin** on Unsplash*

# LESSON 7: BASIC COMMANDS

**Reason**: The basic commands like "sit", "stay", "down", "come", "heel" are not only tricks that will impress your friends but are also **fundamental skills** that all dogs need to have.

Teaching your puppy these basic commands will help **foster better communication** between the two of you and ensure that your pup is both safe and well-behaved.

Just like the commands we've taught in our previous book, these commands will also be very useful for your pup in the big wide world.

**Goal**: Your puppy should be able to **understand and respond** correctly to the basic commands by the end of this training. Each command will be **broken down in detail** in the step-by-step.

**Hint**: Training should **always be a positive experience for your puppy**. Always reward good behaviour with **treats, praise, or play. Remember, patience is key**, puppies learn at their own pace.

Keep training sessions short but consistent to ensure your pup **doesn't get bored or overwhelmed**.

In this section, we will guide you on **how to teach your puppy** these important commands. **Remember**, training should be fun for both of you, so make sure you keep a **positive attitude** and have plenty of treats handy!

The learning process can take some time, but with **consistent training and positive reinforcement**, your puppy will be able to master these commands.

**Step-by-Step**

1. **"Sit" Command:**
   Hold a treat close to your puppy's nose.
   **Move your hand up, allowing their head to follow the treat and causing their bottom to lower.**
   **Once they're in sitting position, say "sit," give them the treat and share affection.**

2. **"Stay" Command:**
   Ask your puppy to "sit."
   **Open the palm of your hand in front of you, and say "stay."**
   **Take a few steps back. Reward them with a treat and affection if they stay.**
   **Gradually increase the number of steps you take before giving the treat.**

3. **"Down" Command:**
   Find a particularly good-smelling treat, and hold it in your closed fist.
   **Hold your hand up to your puppy's snout. When they sniff it, move your hand to the floor, so they follow.**
   **Slide your hand along the ground in front of them to encourage their body to follow their head.**
   **Once they're in the down position, say "down," give them the treat, and share affection.**

4. **"Come" Command:**
   Put a leash and collar on your puppy.
   **Go down to their level and say "come," while gently**

**pulling on the leash.**
**When they get to you, reward them with affection and a treat.**

5. **"Heel" Command:**
   Begin the training session with your puppy on your left side.
   **With a treat in your left hand, say "heel," and start walking.**
   **Keep the treat at your puppy's nose level and allow them to sniff and nibble at it as you walk.**
   **After a few steps, stop and if your puppy is still at your side, praise them and give them the treat.**
   **Repeat this process, increasing the number of steps each time before giving the treat.**

**Remember**, every puppy learns at a different pace, **so don't get discouraged if your puppy doesn't get it right away**. Practice makes perfect!

Why don't dogs ever play hide and seek with their owners?

Because with all the "sit" and "stay" practice, the owners would win every time!

*Photo by **Kobi Kadosh** on Unsplash*

# LESSON 8: BITE INHIBITION

Introduction

Do you know why puppies bite a lot? It's because they are just like us, **they explore their world with their mouths!**

They are also teething and **need to chew on things** to relieve discomfort.

But that doesn't mean we should let them turn us into chew toys!

Learning bite inhibition helps puppies **understand** how to **control the strength of their bite** and when it is not okay to use their teeth on people or objects they shouldn't be chewing on.

**Reason**: Bite inhibition training is important because it helps your puppy understand that human skin is much more sensitive than the fur-covered bodies of their littermates. If they bite too hard during play, the fun stops! So, **they learn to control their bite**.

This can **also prevent potential accidents** in the future when the dog is fully grown and has much stronger jaws.

**Goal**: Your goal in this lesson is to teach your puppy that **biting too hard means playtime is over.** We want to teach them that **soft mouthing is okay**, but hard bites are not. **Remember**, teaching bite inhibition takes time, so **be patient** with your furry friend!

**Hint**: In this lesson, **we are not** completely stopping your pup from using their mouth, but rather teaching them how to control it. It's normal for puppies to mouth your hand gently. **However**, when they start to apply pressure, that's when we have to intervene.

Patience and consistency is the key.

**Step-by-Step**

### Encourage Gentle Play

Start by initiating a play session with your puppy. You can play with a toy or use your hand to gently play with your puppy. **Remember** to keep the play session **light and fun.**

### React to Biting

The moment your puppy bites too hard, let out a high-pitched yelp or say "ouch!" in a firm voice. This is similar to how a puppy would react if a sibling bit them too hard during play. **It's a language they understand**.

### Pause Playtime

After you yelp or say "ouch," **stop the play session immediately**. Turn your back on your puppy and ignore them for about 20-30 seconds. This timeout period teaches your puppy that the fun ends when they bite too hard.

### Resume Playtime

After the brief timeout, you can **resume playing with your puppy**. If they bite too hard again, repeat the steps.

### Gradually Lower the Threshold

Over time, start reacting to softer and softer bites. This helps your puppy **understand** that **any pressure applied to human skin is not acceptable**.

## Reward Gentle Play

If your puppy plays without biting or mouths very gently, praise them and give them a treat. You could say "good gentle!" in a happy, positive voice. This **reinforces** the gentle behaviour.

## Offer Appropriate Chew Toys

**Always** have suitable chew toys available for your puppy. When they start biting, guide them towards these toys. This teaches them what is appropriate to chew on and what isn't.

**Remember**, teaching bite inhibition **takes time and consistency**, but it's a **crucial skill for every puppy to learn**.

So don't lose patience and keep practicing!

Puppies are quite a handful and having all the necessary tools at your disposal is very important!

*Photo by **benjamin lehman** on Unsplash*

# LESSON 9: HANDLING AND GROOMING

**Introduction**

Your puppy is a small, fluffy bundle of joy, and it's almost impossible to resist giving them lots of cuddles and pets.

While this is **great for bonding**, it's also an **excellent opportunity** to get your puppy used to being handled and groomed.

This lesson will teach you how to handle your puppy correctly and **introduce them to grooming tools**.

**Reason**: Getting **your puppy used to being touched and handled can make trips to the vet, grooming sessions, and everyday care a lot easier and less stressful** for both of you. It's much easier to examine, groom, or treat a dog that is **comfortable** with being handled.

**Goal**: Your goal is to make your puppy **feel safe and comfortable** during handling and grooming sessions. You want them to associate these sessions with **positive feelings**, so they're calm and relaxed whenever they're handled in the future.

**Hint**: Remember that handling and grooming should always be a positive experience for your puppy. **Don't rush, and don't force** your puppy if they're feeling uncomfortable. Use plenty of praise, treats, and love to make the experience as positive as possible.

**Step-by-Step**

### Start Slowly

Begin by gently touching and petting your puppy **all over their body** during calm and quiet times. Be sure to touch their paws, ears, tail, and belly.

### Introduce the Tools

Once your puppy seems comfortable with being touched, you can start introducing them to grooming tools. **Show them the tools, let them sniff and investigate**. Give them a treat when they show interest but don't react fearfully.

### First Brushing

Start with a soft brush and gently brush their fur. **Talk to them in a soft, reassuring voice** while you do this. **Again**, give them treats during and after the session.

### Paw Handling

Paws are a **sensitive area** for dogs. Begin by **gently touching** your puppy's paws without holding them. Gradually, as your puppy becomes comfortable, you can start holding their paws, pressing their pads gently, and touching their nails. This will be **important for nail trims in the future.**

### Ear and Mouth Checks

Similar to the paws, start by gently touching your puppy's ears and mouth. **Reward calm behaviour** with treats and praise. **Over time**, try lifting their lips to check their teeth and gums and look inside their ears.

## Bath Time

The first bath can be a big event for a puppy! Make sure the water is warm, **not hot**, and use a **puppy-specific shampoo**. Keep the experience positive with lots of praise and treats.

## Consistency is Key

Repeat these handling and grooming sessions regularly. This will help your puppy **get used to them** and reduce their stress and fear.

**Remember**, patience is key!

You're not only grooming your puppy but also building trust. **Keep the sessions short and positive**, and soon enough, your puppy will be a pro at handling and grooming!

Handling and grooming is an important part of taking care of a dog, **no matter their age**.

If you've been practicing with your grown-up furry friend, now it's time to do the same with your new puppy!

You'll find this very similar to the *'Brushing the Fur'* Super Fun Game you played before! But **remember**, handling includes not just brushing but also checking their ears, teeth, and paws.

*Photo by **Aditya Joshi** on Unsplash*

# LESSON 10: PREVENTING RESOURCE GUARDING

**Introduction**

Resource guarding is a **behavior** that can develop in dogs who feel the need to protect their belongings, such as toys, food, or even their favorite spot on the couch.

**It's essential to address this issue** as early as possible to ensure that your puppy grows up to be a well-behaved and friendly dog.

**Reason**: Dogs can guard their resources due to **instinctual behaviors derived from their ancestors** in the wild. In the modern world, this instinctual behavior can lead to **conflict, aggression, and safety concerns** for both dogs and humans.

As a result, **preventing resource guarding is an important part of a puppy's training.**

**Goal**: The goal is to teach your puppy that they **don't need to guard their resources** and that giving up something doesn't mean they'll lose it forever. We want to create a **positive association with you approaching or touching their things**.

**Hint**: Remember to **be patient**. It's natural for dogs to want to protect their belongings. This training should always be **a positive experience** for your puppy.

**Step by Step**

### Choose a low-value item:

Start with an item your puppy doesn't value highly, **like a less favorite toy**.

### Approach and treat

Walk towards your puppy while they have the item, and toss them a high-value treat, then walk away.

### Repeat

Repeat this process several times until your puppy seems **happy and relaxed** when you approach.

### Upgrade the item

Once your puppy is comfortable with you approaching while they have a low-value item, **repeat the process** with a higher-value item, **like a favorite toy**.

### Touch and treat

Once your puppy is **comfortable** with you approaching them while they have a high-value item, start to **gently** touch the item before giving the treat.

### Take and give

After a few touch-and-treat sessions, try **taking the item away** while giving the treat, and then **immediately** give the item back.

### Repeat with other items and situations

As your puppy becomes comfortable with you taking their items and giving them back, repeat the process with **different**

**items and in various situations**.

**Remember**, the objective is to make your puppy feel that you approaching their resources is a good thing because it results in delicious treats.

**Always** be patient and move at your puppy's pace. If at any point your puppy seems uncomfortable or shows signs of stress, **take a step back and try again later**.

*Photo by **Kelly Sikkema** on Unsplash*

# LESSON 11: ALONE TIME TRAINING

**Introduction**

Puppies are social animals who love being around their humans. **However**, there will be times when they need to be comfortable being alone.

This training helps prevent separation anxiety and promotes independence.

**Reason**: Ensuring that your puppy can spend some **time alone without stress or anxiety is crucial** for their overall well-being and development. It's also important to **prevent potential problems** that may arise when left alone, like excessive barking, destructive behavior, or accidents in the house.

**Goal**: The goal of alone-time training is to teach your puppy **to be comfortable and relaxed when left alone**, and understand that you will always return.

**Hint**: Always ensure that the puppy is safe during their alone time. Use a crate or **puppy-proof area** where they can't get into trouble or hurt themselves.

**Step by Step**

## Start Small

**Begin with very short periods of alone time**. This could be as short as a few seconds to a minute.

## Create a Safe Space

Set up a comfortable and secure area for your puppy, such as a crate or a puppy-proofed room. Place their **favourite toys, a cozy bed, and some water inside**.

## Introduce the Space

Allow your puppy to **explore** the safe space with you there. Reward them with praise and treats for going into the space.

## Increase Time Gradually

Start leaving your puppy in the safe space for **short periods**, gradually increasing the duration. Initially, you might just step out of the room and immediately return.

## Praise Calm Behavior

When you return, if your puppy has remained calm, give them plenty of praise and do not forget a treat.

## Increase Your Distance

As your puppy becomes more comfortable, **start going further away** during their alone time, perhaps even stepping outside the house for a **few minutes**.

## Build up Duration

**Gradually** extend the amount of time your puppy spends alone.

**This should be done over weeks and months, not days.**

## Create Positive Associations

Ensure to provide your puppy with fun toys and treats during their alone time to create a **positive association**.

**Remember**, take your time with this process.

The aim is to ensure your puppy feels safe and secure when left alone, and rushing can lead to fear and anxiety.

Always end on a positive note, **and never use the safe space as a punishment**.

*Photo by **Matthew Henry** on Unsplash*

# SOCIALIZATION AND HABITUATION

**Congratulations**! You have made it through the **'Basic Training'** section.

As we delve deeper into 'Socialization and Habituation', **remember** that if you ever wish to explore a specific topic in more detail, you can easily **refer to the Contents section** to navigate to any particular section of your interest. Your journey through understanding your canine companion continues!

Now, it's time to focus on helping your puppy become a **well-adjusted and well-mannered** member of your family and society. This will be achieved through socialization and habituation, **two critical components** of raising a happy, confident, and well-behaved dog.

## *What is Socialization?*

Socialization is the action of introducing your puppy to a **wide variety of experiences**, including **different environments, people, animals, and sounds**. This helps them understand that these experiences are normal and nothing to be afraid of.

Well-socialized puppies generally **grow into confident, secure dogs** who are comfortable in various situations.

## *What is Habituation?*

Habituation is the process of getting your **puppy used to the everyday things** they will encounter in their lives, like the sound of the vacuum cleaner, the sight of a stroller, or the hustle and bustle on a city street. Habituation helps puppies **learn to ignore these common stimuli,** so they don't react to them with fear or aggression.

**Remember**, in our previous book *"Puppy Training 101: A Practical Guide for Young Dog Owners,"* we touched on the importance of understanding your **dog's body language**. The same applies here.

Pay close attention to your **puppy's body language** during socialization and habituation to ensure they're comfortable and not overly stressed.

Take things slow, make sure each new experience is positive, and always **let your puppy dictate the pace**.

In the upcoming section, we'll dive into the various elements of socialization and habituation, including meeting new people and animals, **exposing your puppy to different environments**, sounds, and experiences, and helping them become comfortable with common household activities.

Your role is not just to expose your puppy to these things, but to help them develop a **positive association** with them. So, always pair new experiences with positive reinforcements like treats, toys, and praise.

Stay tuned!

The journey toward raising a well-rounded puppy continues!

*Photo by **Mia Anderson** on Unsplash*

# 1. UNDERSTANDING SOCIALIZATION AND HABITUATION

Welcome to the world of puppy socialization and habituation!

**These are two big words, but don't worry, they're not as complicated as they might sound.** They are fundamental concepts in puppy training that can help shape a well-rounded, friendly, and confident dog.

**Socialization** is all about introducing your puppy to a variety of experiences, people, environments, other animals, and situations. It's essentially **getting your puppy used to the world around them**.

The goal of socialization is to help your puppy **feel comfortable and secure in different circumstances**, minimizing the risk of fear, aggression, or anxiety later on in life.

Imagine if you were taken to a new planet where everything was different - the people, the animals, the scenery, even the

50

sounds. It would be pretty scary, right? Now, think about how a puppy might feel coming into our world. **They have so much to learn and so much to get used to!**

That's why socialization is so important.

**Habituation**, on the other hand, is the process of **helping your puppy get used to things they will encounter on a regular basis**, so they become a normal part of life for your dog. This includes everyday household noises like the vacuum cleaner or doorbell, and routines like bathing and feeding times.

Habituation aims to make these **regular occurrences so common to your puppy** that they hardly notice them at all.

Both **socialization and habituation should start as early as possible**.

In fact, your puppy's most critical socialization period is between 3 and 12-14 weeks old, a time frame often called the **'Socialization Window.'** This is the age when puppies are most receptive to learning about their world. So, the experiences they have during this time can **greatly influence their personality and behavior** in the future.

**Remember**, the world can be an exciting but sometimes scary place for a puppy, just like in our first book, "Puppy Training 101: A Practical Guide for Young Dog Owners". With patience, consistency, and a lot of love, we can help our puppies navigate it with confidence.

**Stay tuned** as we delve into the different areas of socialization and habituation and provide practical tips and tricks to help you on this exciting journey.

It's going to be a fun ride!

*Photo by **Justin Veenema** on Unsplash*

# 2. PEOPLE SOCIALIZATION

Hooray, we're starting with people socialization!

This is a **fun and rewarding** part of your puppy's training journey.

The goal of people socialization is **to help your puppy feel comfortable and confident around different types of people**. After all, our world is filled with all sorts of wonderful individuals, and we want our puppies to feel at ease with everyone they meet.

Let's begin with an important reminder: **every puppy is unique**.

**Just like us**, some may be extroverts who are eager to make friends, while others might be a bit shy or anxious around new people. And that's perfectly okay! **It's our job** as humans to help them navigate these encounters at their own pace.

Start by introducing your puppy to the people in your immediate household.

**Remember**, these introductions should **always be positive and stress-free**.

Let your puppy approach new people **on their own terms**. Encourage **gentle** handling and use treats to make these encounters rewarding.

**Next**, broaden your puppy's social circle to include a variety of people.

Think about all the different people your pup might encounter throughout their life - men, women, children, elderly individuals, people with hats or sunglasses, people using walking aids, postmen, delivery people, and the list goes on.

**Remember** the key rule: **take it slow**. We don't want to overwhelm our puppies. Gradual, **positive exposure is the way to go.**

Here's **a step-by-step** guide to people socialization:

### Step 1: Start with one new person at a time

Have this person approach calmly, **without direct eye contact** (which can be intimidating for a puppy).

### Step 2: Let your puppy make the first move.

It's important they feel they have control over the situation.

### Step 3: Encourage the new person

Ask the new person to offer your puppy a treat or a favourite toy. This will create a **positive association** with meeting new people.

### Step 4: Once your puppy is comfortable

Allow the new person to **gently pet your puppy**, starting from their chest or side (avoid reaching over their head initially as it can be scary for them).

### Step 5: Repeat

Repeat these steps with different people, **remembering** to keep the experiences positive.

## *Step 6: More people*

Gradually increase the number of people your puppy meets at once, and the variety of people they interact with.

Finally, **remember** to have fun! People socialization is not just an essential part of training, it's also an opportunity for your puppy **to learn that the world is a friendly and exciting place**.

A **positive attitude and patience are key** in any training process.

So, let's embrace this adventure **with lots of love and positivity!**

*Photo by **Bruce Warrington** on Unsplash*

# 3. ANIMAL SOCIALIZATION

Yay, it's **time for your puppy to make some furry friends!**

The world of animal socialization is so exciting - imagine all the fun your puppy will have meeting other dogs, cats, and even different animals. In this part of our guide, we'll show you how to help your puppy **develop positive relationships** with other animals.

**Remember**, your puppy is an individual with their own personality. Just like us, some may be more social and playful, while others may prefer a quiet snuggle with their humans. And that's okay! **We're here to guide them** through the socialization process at their own pace.

The first step is to safely introduce your puppy **to other vaccinated dogs**. This could be with a neighbour's dog or at a controlled puppy socialization class.

The goal is to let your puppy learn dog-to-dog communication in a **safe and supportive environment.**

During these interactions, **always supervise** and keep playtime balanced. Watch out for signs of **stress or fear** in your puppy or the other dogs.

Remember, **it's all about positive experiences!**

Next, broaden your puppy's social experiences to **include a variety of animals**. This could include cats, birds, or even livestock if you live in a rural area.

Here's our **step-by-step** guide to animal socialization:

### Step 1: Start with a calm and well-socialized adult dog

Your puppy can learn a lot from a gentle and patient doggy mentor!

### Step 2: Dogs on a leash at first

Keep both dogs on a leash at first, and let them sniff and explore each other at their own pace. **Reward positive interactions** with treats or praise.

### Step 3: Increase the time

Gradually increase the time they spend together, **always under supervision**.

### Step 4: Repeat

Repeat this process with other dogs, always ensuring they are vaccinated and **friendly**.

### Step 5: Different animals

For introducing other types of animals, use the same gradual approach. Keep both animals **under control** to ensure their safety.

Animal socialization is such a beautiful journey. By guiding your puppy through these experiences, you're helping them to **become a confident and well-rounded** dog. And who knows, they might even make some lifelong friends along the way!

Approach this process **with love, patience, and a big smile!**

Note by the publisher: From the same author, if you are

looking for a comprehensive look at the **fascinating world of dog-human dialogue**, and an insightful exploration into how we can better appreciate our four-legged friends, embark on an eye-opening journey into the fascinating world of dog-human communications with the book *"Dog Speak: Exploring Dog-Human Dialogue and AI's Future Role"*

Also our insightful guide, *"The Harmonious Household: Your Step-by-Step Guide to Introducing Cats and Dogs"*. This comprehensive resource demystifies the process of helping your beloved pets live together harmoniously. It's crafted with the same dedication and expertise that went into this book, and *"Puppy Training 101: A Practical Guide for Young Dog Owners"*. Dive into a treasure trove of wisdom about **understanding dog-cat dynamics**, preparation before introduction, observing interactions, and managing common challenges. Designed to turn your home into a **peaceful pet paradise**, this guide is a must-read for any pet parent navigating the world of multi-species cohabitation. Written with warmth and wit by Max Biscuit, it's your roadmap to a harmonious home.

See the "Books By This Author" section at the end of this book for the complete list.

*Photo by Ruby Schmank on Unsplash*

# 4. ENVIRONMENTAL SOCIALIZATION

The world is one **giant playground** for your puppy, filled with sights, smells, and sounds just waiting to be explored!

Through environmental socialization, we can guide our puppies **to understand and feel comfortable in the world around them.** In this section, we'll dive into the exciting process of environmental socialization and offer tips on how to navigate this important stage.

We've talked a lot about socializing with people and other animals, but what about everything else that **makes up a puppy's world?**

Things like car rides, the sound of a vacuum cleaner, and the feel of different types of flooring under their paws – **all these can be new experiences for a puppy**.

**Environmental socialization** involves exposing your puppy to different environments, sounds, objects, and experiences **in a positive and controlled manner**. By doing so, you're helping your puppy to **build confidence and reduce fear or anxiety**

towards new experiences.

Start in your own home by exposing your puppy to various household noises and objects.

From the hairdryer to the washing machine, these can all be strange new experiences for a puppy! **Remember to pair each new experience with something positive**, like a treat or a cuddle, to help them build **positive associations**.

From there, take your puppy out on adventures. Let them explore **different textures** under their paws, like grass, concrete, sand, and gravel. Expose them to **different weather conditions** like rain, snow, and sunshine. Take them on a **car ride** or a trip to a pet-friendly store.

**Step-by-Step**

## Step 1: Start at home

Start in a familiar environment – your home! **Gradually** introduce your puppy to different rooms, objects, and household sounds.

## Step 2: Make it positive

Pair each new experience with **something positive**, such as a treat or praise. This will help your puppy to build positive associations.

## Step 3: Excursion

**Gradually** take your puppy on outings to different environments, like parks, pet-friendly stores, or a short car ride.

## Step 4: Be attentive

**Always** observe your puppy's reactions. If they show signs of fear or anxiety, reduce the intensity of the experience, and offer comfort and reassurance.

## Step 5: Repeat

Repeat this process consistently, gradually exposing your puppy to new experiences over time.

**Remember**, every puppy is unique and will react differently to various stimuli. Always **go at your puppy's pace**, and never force an experience if your puppy seems scared or overwhelmed.

Let's emphasize the importance of **patience and understanding**.

Carry these principles forward as you guide your puppy through this exciting world of new experiences.

Happy exploring!

*Photo by **Viktoria Lavrynenko** on **Unsplash***

# 5. SENSORY SOCIALIZATION

Welcome to the amazing world of sensory socialization!

This area of puppy training is about helping your furry friend become **accustomed to different sensations. Sight, smell, sound, touch, and even taste** – we'll touch on each of these as we navigate this fascinating process together.

Ready? Let's get started!

Puppies are **incredibly curious** creatures, eager to explore the world with **their noses, mouths, eyes, ears, and paws**. As pet owners, we have the exciting opportunity to guide them through this discovery process, ensuring they build positive associations along the way.

In the same way that we helped our puppies explore different environments in the previous section, sensory socialization encourages them to **experience various sensory stimuli**.

This could be anything from the sound of a siren, to the feel of grass under their paws, to the smell of different foods.

Here's a **step-by-step** guide to sensory socialization:

### Step 1: Begin with gentle exposure

You can **start at home**, using everyday household items and noises to stimulate your puppy's senses. Let them feel different textures, hear various sounds, and smell diverse scents.

### Step 2: Make it positive

**Pair** each new sensory experience with something positive. Treats, praise, or a favourite toy work wonders for **creating positive associations**.

### Step 3: Increase intensity

**Gradually** increase the intensity of the sensory experiences. For example, if you're working on sound socialization, you can gradually increase the volume or change the types of sound your puppy is exposed to.

### Step 4: Monitor your puppy's reactions closely

**Remember**, we want these experiences to be positive and not scary. If your puppy seems uncomfortable, **reduce the intensity** of the stimulus and reassure them.

### Step 5: Repeat

Repeat and **diversify** these sensory experiences over time. **Consistency is key** in helping your puppy become comfortable with various sensory stimuli.

Sensory socialization is **an ongoing process**, and it's important to keep exposing your puppy to different experiences throughout their life. This doesn't have to be complicated – **even a walk in the park** can expose your puppy to new sights, smells, and sounds.

**Remember, training is a journey**, not a race.

It's about building a strong, positive relationship with your puppy.

So **have patience, make it fun**, and enjoy this sensory adventure together.

Happy socializing!

*Photo by **Wai Siew** on **Unsplash***

# 6. HANDLING AND GROOMING HABITUATION

Hello to all budding puppy trainers and handlers out there!

Today, we are focusing on something that **might seem simple** but is essential to a smooth life with your puppy - handling and grooming habituation.

Excited to learn more? Let's dive right in!

Just like humans, puppies also need to get used to being touched and groomed.

Think about it - how would you feel if you had never had a haircut, and someone suddenly came at you with a pair of scissors? Scary, right? **That's why, it's important we take time to help our puppies get used to handling and grooming activities**.

Here's a **step-by-step** guide on how to make handling and grooming a pleasant experience for your puppy:

## Step 1: Start with a gentle touch

It can be as simple as petting your puppy, stroking their fur, or massaging their paws. These actions not only help them get used to being handled but also **help you build a strong bond** with your puppy.

### Step 2: Slowly introduce grooming tools

Start with a soft brush and gently brush your puppy's fur. Make sure to pair this new experience with treats and praise to **create positive associations**.

### Step 3: Gradually increase the complexity

As your puppy gets comfortable with simple grooming, you can introduce more complex activities such as nail clipping, ear cleaning, or teeth brushing. **Remember**, go slow, and reward your puppy after each session.

### Step 4: Different scenarios

Get your puppy used to different handling scenarios. Lift them (carefully, of course), flip them onto their back, and examine their ears, mouth, and paws. This will **help them get used to being handled** by a vet or a professional groomer in the future.

### Step 5: Always be gentle and patient

If your puppy seems uncomfortable or scared at any point, **stop what you're doing**, and go back to a simpler step. **Remember**, the aim is to make handling and grooming a positive experience.

We do emphasize **that patience is key in puppy training**.

With time and consistency, your puppy will learn to stay calm during handling and grooming sessions. It's not just about keeping your puppy looking good, it's about **teaching them to trust and bond with you**.

So, let's pick up that brush and turn grooming time into fun time!

Happy handling and grooming!

*Photo by **Michelle Tresemer** on Unsplash*

# 7. HABITUATION TO HOUSEHOLD ACTIVITIES

**Greetings, aspiring dog trainers and caregivers!**

It's time to dive into another exciting aspect of raising a puppy – **getting them used to everyday household activities**. Are you ready to make your house a comfortable, exciting, and safe place for your furry friend?

Let's get started!

The home is a busy place with various activities always taking place. To us, these activities are mundane, but **for a puppy, they're all new experiences**.

The hum of the refrigerator, the spin of the washing machine, the clatter of pots and pans in the kitchen, the beeping of the microwave - these are **all sounds and activities** that your puppy **needs to get accustomed to**.

**But don't worry,** with patience and consistent efforts, your puppy will soon feel right at home amidst all the hustle and bustle.

Here are some steps to help you along the way:

## Step 1: Gradual Exposure

Start by exposing your puppy to the sights and sounds of your home in a gradual, non-threatening way. Keep their first encounters with new noises and sights **short and positive**. The goal here is to make them understand that these activities are a normal part of life and nothing to be scared of.

## Step 2: Pair with Positive Reinforcement

When exposing your puppy to new household sounds and sights, pair it with treats, praises, or cuddles. This will help your puppy associate these activities with **positive feelings.**

## Step 3: Incorporate into Routine

Make exposure to household activities **a part of your puppy's daily routine**. This could be as simple as having them sit in the kitchen while you cook or in the laundry room while you do the washing.

## Step 4: Be Patient

**Remember**, it's all new for your puppy, and it might take some time for them to get used to all the noises and movements.

**Be patient**, and do not force them to face their fears. Instead, let them take their time to explore and understand the environment at their own pace.

**Every puppy is unique**, and they will adapt to their new environment at their own speed.

**Don't forget**, the goal here is to make your puppy feel comfortable and safe in their new home.

**This isn't a race, so take it slow**, and enjoy the process. In the end, seeing your puppy confidently exploring their surroundings and calmly dealing with the daily hustle and bustle will be worth every effort. So, ready to start?

Let's make your home a happy place for your new buddy!

*Photo by JC Gellidon on Unsplash*

# 8. PREVENTING FEAR AND PHOBIAS

Hello again, dear friends and fellow puppy-raisers!

Now that your new pal is getting accustomed to household activities, sights, and sounds, it's time to address an important aspect of **their mental well-being**.

Today, we'll talk about preventing fears and phobias in your young canine companion. As always, **patience and positivity will be key** in this part of your journey together.

As we all know, **fear is a natural and necessary response to potential dangers.**

However, when fear becomes excessive, irrational, or pervasive, it **can develop into a phobia** that can seriously impair your puppy's quality of life.

This is **why it's crucial that we understand the nature of fears and phobias** and take proactive steps to prevent them from developing in our young furry friends.

So, how can we do that?

**Here are some effective steps:**

### Step 1: Early and Positive Experiences

The world is full of new and strange things for a puppy. It's crucial to make sure that their **initial experiences** with new people, animals, environments, and situations are **positive**. In the previous sections, we've discussed in detail how to provide these positive experiences, and **they all apply here too!**

### Step 2: Understanding Your Puppy's Body Language

Your puppy may not be able to speak words, but **they have a language of their own**.

Pay **close attention** to your puppy's body language. Signs of fear can include cowering, tail tucking, yawning, excessive panting, or trying to escape. If you notice these signs, it's important to **remove your puppy from the situation** causing fear and gradually reintroduce it in a more controlled and comforting way.

### Step 3: Gradual Desensitization

If your puppy exhibits fear towards a specific object, sound, or situation, **gradually** expose them to it in a non-threatening way. **Start at a low intensity** and gradually increase it as your puppy becomes more comfortable. For instance, if your puppy is afraid of loud noises, start with a quieter version of the noise and gradually increase the volume over time.

### Step 4: Positive Reinforcement

Always reward your puppy's courage. If they confront a fear or show any signs of overcoming it, **immediately** offer them praise, cuddles, and their favorite treats. This positive reinforcement will **encourage them to face their fears**.

### Step 5: Consult a Professional

If you find your puppy's fear persisting despite your best efforts, **do not hesitate** to consult a professional dog trainer or instead a veterinary behaviourist. They can provide more specialized guidance based on **your puppy's specific needs**.

**Remember**, understanding dog behaviour and communication is key.

The journey towards preventing fears and phobias in your puppy can be challenging, **but with patience, understanding, and love, you can help them grow into a confident and happy dog**.

So, let's get started, shall we?

The world is waiting for your brave, little explorer!

*Photo by Jametlene Reskp on Unsplash*

# 9. SOCIALIZATION SCHEDULE

Hello again, my fellow puppy trainers and lovers! Are you ready for the next exciting step in your journey with your new best friend?

We're going to create a socialization schedule together, to ensure **your puppy gets the exposure they need during their crucial developmental period.**

**Remember**, successful socialization can be one of the **greatest gifts** you can give to your furry friend, so let's dive in!

## *Week 8-10: Family Time and Home Exploration*

This is when your puppy starts exploring their new home, meeting all the family members, and getting used to the household environment. Make sure **all family interactions are gentle, positive, and respectful**.

Let your puppy **explore** the different rooms, garden (if you have one), and encounter common household noises like the vacuum cleaner, washing machine, and television.

### Week 10-12: Expanding Their World

Once your puppy has had their vaccinations, it's time to gradually introduce them to **the world outside**. Start with short walks around the neighbourhood, letting them get used to new sounds, smells, and sights.

Introduce them to friendly neighbours and let them see other animals from a safe distance. Remember, **all new experiences should be positive** and non-threatening.

### Week 12-16: New People, Animals, and Environments

Now that your puppy is getting more comfortable in the outside world, it's time to introduce them to **new people, animals, and environments**.

Arrange playdates with **other vaccinated dogs**, take them to busy parks to observe different people and animals, and expose them to various environments like pet-friendly stores, lakes, or forests. Continue to **reinforce positive behaviours** with treats and praises.

### Week 16-20: Public Transportation and Advanced Situations

If possible, introduce your puppy to different modes of transportation **like cars**, buses, or trains. Also, start training your puppy to handle more advanced situations. For example, you could have them encounter **people with umbrellas, people on bicycles, or noisy traffic**.

Keep all experiences positive, **and do not force your puppy** if they show signs of fear or discomfort.

### Month 6 onwards: Maintenance and Continued Exposure

After your puppy is 6 months old, continue to expose

them to **diverse situations, people, and environments**. Attend puppy training classes, visit dog-friendly cafes or markets, and **maintain regular playdates**. The goal is to keep their socialization skills sharp and their experiences varied.

**Remember, every puppy is unique**, and some might take longer to be comfortable in new situations.

**Be patient** and never force your puppy into a situation they find distressing. **It's not a race**, but a journey, and the goal is to make your puppy a well-adjusted and confident adult dog.

Creating a successful socialization schedule for your puppy might seem like a big task, but **remember**, it's an exciting and rewarding journey.

You're not just training your puppy; you're creating memories and strengthening the bond with your new best friend.

**So let's enjoy the journey together!**

# 10. SOCIALIZATION AND COVID-19

Greetings, brave and dedicated puppy trainers!

We're living in unique times, and while the COVID-19 pandemic has affected many areas of our lives, we need to ensure it **doesn't hinder the socialization process** of our little furry companions.

You might think it's challenging, but believe me, **with a little creativity**, we can turn this situation into an opportunity for fun and bonding.

Let's discover how!

## 1. Adapt to the New Normal

First things first, **remember** that dogs are extremely adaptable creatures. They can adjust to new circumstances, and with our guidance, **they can even thrive**. With that said, COVID-19 restrictions may have limited our usual socialization methods, but they haven't eradicated them entirely.

## 2. Indoor Socialization

You might be spending more time indoors, but **that doesn't mean socialization has to halt**. Expose your puppy to different household sights, sounds, and smells.

**Remember** the vacuum cleaner, washing machine, and television we talked about in the socialization schedule? These are all great ways to help your puppy adjust to everyday life.

## 3. The Power of Technology

**Technology** can be a valuable asset for puppy socialization. Video calls with friends and family can introduce your puppy to different faces and voices. They can even meet **other pets through the screen**!

While it's not the same as face-to-face interaction, it can still be a valuable tool in their socialization journey.

## 4. Outdoor Exploration

**Even during the pandemic,** outdoor exercise is essential for your dog's physical and mental well-being. Short walks while maintaining social distancing can introduce your puppy to a wealth of new experiences.

The feel of different terrains under their paws, the smell of fresh air, the sight of birds and squirrels – these are **all crucial elements** of their environmental socialization.

## 5. Social Distancing Socializing

When out for walks, you might come across other dog owners. Even while maintaining a **safe distance**, your puppy can learn a lot from observing other dogs and humans.

This can be a good way of introducing them to the concept that other dogs and people exist without necessarily having to interact with them physically.

## 6. Online Training Classes

With the pandemic, many **dog training classes** have moved online. These classes not only teach your puppy basic commands, but also help them get used to seeing different people and dogs, albeit on a screen.

## 7. Creativity is Key

Use this time as an opportunity **to be creative with your puppy's socialization**.

Build obstacle courses at home, introduce them to various toys and puzzles, play different types of music, or even dance with them. These experiences **will enrich their world** and help them become well-rounded dogs.

**Always remember**, the bond you and your puppy develop during this time will be unique and special.

**You're not just a trainer** to your puppy; you're their guide, their protector, and most importantly, their best friend.

Times like this are tough, but together, you and your puppy can face anything. After all, **every cloud has a silver lining!**

So even when times are tough, remember - **you're doing a great job**, and your puppy is lucky to have you!

**Keep up the good work!**

*Photo by **Phil Botha** on Unsplash*

# NAME RECOGNITION

**Hello**, future professional puppy trainers!

Now that we've covered the broad strokes of understanding dog behaviour, socialization, and habituation, it's time to get down to some of the more specific training, starting with **one of the most critical early lessons** for your furry friend: **Name Recognition**.

**Learning their name is the first step towards your puppy understanding and responding to more complex commands**. It's the **foundational** piece that makes all other training easier and more efficient.

After all, every great conversation begins with someone's name, doesn't it?

## *Why is Name Recognition Important?*

Just like we respond when someone calls our name, teaching your puppy to respond to theirs can be **very helpful**. It can help get their attention during training, call them back to you in the park, or redirect their attention from something they shouldn't be investigating.

## Choosing the Right Name

**Before we start**, let's address the name itself.

You might be thinking, **"But we've already named our puppy!"** That's great! But let's ensure it's a name conducive to training.

**Short, distinct names** that don't sound like common commands tend to work best. It helps prevent confusion. For instance, "Kit" might sound a lot like "Sit" to a puppy. **More on this later**.

## The Training Process

The process for teaching name recognition is relatively straightforward.

However, like everything worthwhile, it requires **consistency, patience, and positive reinforcement**. It's the mantra we keep reverting to, isn't it? It's because these are indeed the **cornerstones** of any successful training program.

You'll be glad to know that we've covered a step-by-step guide to name recognition training in <u>Lesson 3 of the Basic Training section</u>. Go over it, and remember, **practice makes perfect**.

It might take a few days, or even a few weeks, but trust the process and keep it fun and engaging for your puppy.

## A Word of Caution

One essential point to remember is **not to overuse your puppy's name** or use it when you're frustrated or angry. You want your puppy to associate their name with good things, not negativity. Their name should be a call to attention and positive interaction, **not a signal for punishment or scolding**.

**Remember**, all the guidance, steps, and techniques for name recognition and more are in our first book, *"Puppy Training 101: A Practical Guide for Young Dog Owners"*. It's an excellent resource to fall back upon when in doubt.

Training your puppy is not just about teaching them good manners. It's about **building a bond of mutual respect and understanding**.

So, let's start calling our puppies by their names and let them learn to love the sound of it!

*Photo by **Pauline Loroy** on Unsplash*

# 1. INTRODUCTION TO NAME RECOGNITION

**Welcome back**, young trainers and grown-ups!

It's exciting to see you here again, ready to embark on another delightful journey of training with your fluffy pal.

Today, we're diving into **an essential, foundational piece of puppy training: Name Recognition.** In this book, **we'll delve even deeper, exploring new insights and methods** that will transform your puppy into a responsive and attentive friend.

**What's in a name, you ask?**

Well, for a puppy, their name is more than just a tag; **it's an attention grabber, an identifier, and a bridge that connects their tiny, bustling world to yours.** When your puppy learns their name, they understand that when you call it, you're looking for them. You're not just making noise; **you want their attention.**

The **whole concept of training hinges upon this vital step—** getting your pup to focus on you at the sound of their name.

Teaching your puppy their name is one of the very first steps you will take together, a gentle introduction into **the world of training**.

This process **is fun and bonding**, sprinkled with tiny victories that will make you swell with pride. The moment your puppy turns their little head upon hearing their name, **it's not just a sign of understanding; it's a sign of trust, a proof of the bond that's forming between the two of you**.

Moreover, name recognition is **the foundation for all other commands**.

Whether you're teaching your puppy to sit, stay, or come, it always starts with their name. A well-trained pup who responds to their name **is also safer**. In potential danger situations, like a nearby busy street or a sudden storm, **calling their name** can get them to focus on you, and with further training, get them to come back to you.

This chapter is **your ultimate guide** to teaching your puppy to understand and respond to their name.

And don't worry; we've made sure it's **packed with plenty of tips, techniques, and fun activities** that make the learning process enjoyable for both you and your new best buddy.

So, are you ready to hear the magical sound of your puppy responding to their name?

**Excellent!** Let's turn the page and start this wonderful adventure.

*Photo by **freestocks** on Unsplash*

# 2. CHOOSING THE RIGHT NAME

Welcome to the first important decision of your puppy parenting journey: choosing the **perfect name** for your fur baby.

This decision is **more than just about what sounds cute or what's trendy**.

As your pup's primary identifier, the name you choose plays a significant role in your puppy's training and, subsequently, their safety.

Here are a few guidelines to **help you pick the right name** for your best friend:

## 1. Easy to Say, Easy to Hear

First off, a practical tip: the name should be easy to say and easy for the dog to distinguish. A one or **two-syllable name typically works best**. They're easy to pronounce, and dogs seem to **respond well to short, crisp names**. Think of names like "Max," "Bella," "Lassie," or "Coco."

## 2. Clear, Distinct Sounds

Dogs don't understand language the same way we do. **They respond to sounds**. When it comes to dog names, the sounds you use matter.

Dogs have an **incredible sense of hearing**. They can pick up frequencies between 40 Hz to 60,000 Hz, or 60 kHz (higher frequency/pitch limit than humans), while humans are only capable of hearing frequencies ranging from 20 Hz to 20,000 Hz, or 20 kHz, means that their keen sense of hearing is why clear, **distinct sounds in their names** can make a difference.

**Here's a closer look.**

### A. Consonants

Certain consonants can help to get your dog's attention. Letters like 's', 'sh', 'ch', 'k', 't', and hard 'c' **are sharp and crisp to a dog's ears**. For example, consider the name "Spike." The sharp 's' sound at the beginning and the hard 'k' sound at the end make it clear and easy for the dog to recognize.

### B. Vowels

Vowel sounds can **also be significant**. Dogs seem to respond well to names that end in a long vowel sound, particularly "a" or "i." For example, "Bella," "Chloe," "Bailey," or "Lassie." The long vowel sounds make these names carry, and they can be **easier for dogs to distinguish** from other sounds in the environment.

### C. Pitch

The pitch of your voice can also impact a dog's ability to recognize their name. Dogs tend to **respond better to higher-pitched voices**. So, when you're calling your dog's name, **a slightly higher and enthusiastic pitch** can help them recognize their name faster.

The key is to make the **name distinct from the ambient noise** of everyday life and the common commands you will use. The easier it is for your puppy to recognize their name, **the faster they'll respond**, making training and everyday communication smoother and more effective.

### 3. Avoid Similarities to Command Words

Avoid names that sound like common command words. For instance, "Kit" might be too similar to "sit," **which can cause confusion for your puppy** during training. It's best to choose a name that's **distinctly different from command words**.

### 4. Reflect Their Personality

Every pup has a **unique personality**. A great way to come up with a name is to observe your puppy's behaviour and characteristics for the first few days. Is your pup adventurous, lazy, goofy, or sweet? **Their personality** can give you clues for the perfect name.

### 5. Make it Timeless

While it's tempting to choose a name that's trendy or inspired by your favourite TV show character, remember that your puppy will grow and their name will stay with them for a lifetime. **Choose a name that you believe you (and they) will be happy with long-term.**

**Remember**, choosing a name is not a race. **Take your time**.

You might need to try out a few names before you find the perfect fit. The **most important thing** is that the name suits your puppy and you like calling it out because you'll be doing a lot of that in the days to come!

**The moment of recognition**, when your puppy first turns their head upon hearing their name, is one of the most rewarding parts of the early days of puppy parenthood.

So choose **wisely**, choose with love, and let the magic unfold.

*Photo by **Cookie the Pom** on Unsplash*

# 3. THE TRAINING PROCESS

Ah, the art of teaching your puppy their name!

This may be one of the **first real training exercises** you embark on with your furry friend, and it is a delightful journey.

Name recognition is not just about calling your dog when it's time for dinner or during a game of fetch; **it's the foundation for all future communication**.

So let's dive into the training process.

## 1. Starting Off

Begin in a **quiet**, familiar environment with **minimal distractions**. It's easier for your puppy to focus on you when they are not competing with too many stimuli. Once your pup gets better at name recognition, you can **slowly introduce more distractions**.

## 2. Positive Association

Remember, your puppy **doesn't know what a "name" is yet**.

When you say their name, **it's initially just a sound to them.** Your objective is to create a **positive association between that**

**sound and your puppy**. Say their name, and as soon as they look at you, praise them enthusiastically and give them a small treat.

This process is called "**charging the name**," and it's a way to make your dog feel good whenever they hear their name.

### 3. Consistency

Consistency is key. Use the **same tone of voice**, and call them by the full name you've chosen - not variations or nicknames. This will help your dog understand that that specific sound is associated with them.

### 4. Repetition

Repeat this process multiple times a day, but keep the training sessions short and sweet (5-10 minutes each time). **Puppies have short attention spans**, and you don't want to tire them out.

### 5. The Three D's

Gradually work on the three D's - **Duration, Distraction, and Distance.**

#### A. Duration
Start by calling their name when they are not busy and are likely to respond. Then gradually call their name when they are slightly distracted, and so on.

#### B. Distraction
As your puppy gets more comfortable, introduce **mild distractions**, and practice in different environments.

#### C. Distance
Begin training close to your puppy. As they get better at responding, **gradually increase the distance** between you when you call their name.

**Remember** to always **end each training session on a positive note**, even if it's just one successful response to their name.

**Celebrate** small victories along the way - this is a process, after all!

Above all, **be patient. Learning takes time**.

**Remember** that every dog is different, and they learn at their own pace.

With **consistent effort** and a whole lot of love, your pup will soon respond to their name like a pro.

**Go to the next page** and start training your puppy to recognize his name.

Happy training!

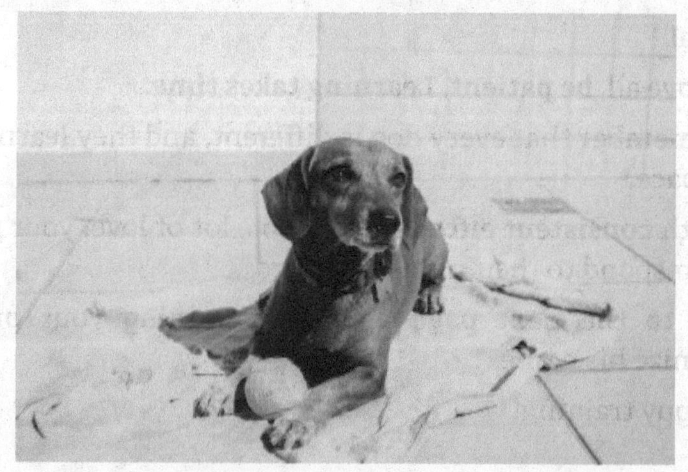

*Photo by **Isabela Kronemberger** on Unsplash*

# 4. STEP-BY-STEP GUIDE TO NAME RECOGNITION TRAINING

So, you've got your puppy's name sorted, and you're ready to get started on the exciting journey of name recognition training.

Below is a simple, step-by-step guide **to help you and your pup** successfully navigate this process together.

## *Step 1: Choose Your Moment*

Start a training session when your **puppy is attentive but not overly excited or tired.** They need to be calm enough to concentrate but lively enough to engage.

Mornings and afternoons are usually great times to train.

## *Step 2: Quiet Space*

Begin in a quiet, familiar space with **minimal distractions.** Too many new sights and sounds can pull your puppy's attention away from you, making the training less effective.

### Step 3: Use Their Name

With a treat in your hand, call your puppy's name in a clear, cheerful voice. Ensure you **use the same tone and pronunciation each time** to avoid confusion.

### Step 4: Reward Their Response

If your puppy turns their head or looks at you when you call their name, **immediately** give them lots of praise and a treat. This helps to reinforce the behaviour you want and **builds a positive association with their name.**

### Step 5: Repeat

Repeat the process multiple times during the session, **but keep it short and sweet**. Puppies have short attention spans, and you want to keep this training fun and engaging.

### Step 6: Gradual Progression

Once your puppy starts consistently responding to their name in a quiet environment, **start adding small distractions** and gradually increase the distance between you.

### Step 7: Patience and Consistency

**Remember,** patience and consistency are key. Some days might be harder than others, **and that's okay**.

If a session doesn't go well, try again later or the next day. **Don't get frustrated or discouraged**; your puppy is learning a new skill, and it takes time.

### Step 8: Daily Practice

Try to practice name recognition **multiple times a day, but only for short periods**. This will keep it enjoyable for your puppy and prevent them from getting bored or frustrated.

### Step 9: The Three D's

Once your puppy has mastered name recognition in a controlled environment, start working on the Three D's: **Duration, Distraction, and Distance**. Gradually increase the duration of their focus, the level of distractions present, and the distance between you and your pup.

**Remember**, training should be fun for both you and your puppy!

**Make sure you're both in a good mood** and ready to enjoy the process. Keep sessions short, positive, and filled with lots of love and praise.

Your puppy will soon be responding to their name like a champion.

**Happy training!**

*Photo by **Victor Grabarczyk** on Unsplash*

# 5. COMMON MISTAKES AND HOW TO AVOID THEM

Training a puppy to recognize their name can be a delightful and rewarding process, but like any training venture, it **comes with potential pitfalls**.

Let's explore **some common mistakes** and how you can sidestep them to ensure a successful and positive training experience.

## 1. Using the Name to Scold

Using your puppy's name **in a negative context**, such as when they're in trouble, can create an **adverse association**. Your pup might associate their name with negative experiences and become hesitant to respond to it.

Avoid this mistake by always using their name in a positive context, **particularly during the training period**.

## 2. Overuse of the Name

Don't turn your puppy's name into background noise by saying it too frequently without purpose. This **can make it**

**lose its impact**. Save it for times when you really need their attention. **Make it special.**

## 3. Expecting Instant Results

Training takes time and patience. **Don't expect** your puppy to consistently respond to their name after just a few tries. It's a learning process for both of you. **Celebrate small victories** and keep a positive mindset.

## 4. Neglecting Practice in Different Environments

Just because your puppy responds to their name at home doesn't mean they'll do the same at the park. **Practice name recognition in various environments** with different levels of distractions.

## 5. Inconsistent Tone and Pronunciation

Your puppy won't understand that "Fido," "Fiiido," and "FIDOOO" are the same name. **Consistency in tone and pronunciation** helps your puppy recognize and respond to their name more quickly.

## 6. Lack of Rewards

Forgetting to reward your puppy when they respond to their name can slow down the training process. **Remember, positive reinforcement accelerates learning**. Whether it's a treat, praise, or a belly rub, make sure to reward your pup **each time they respond to their name.**

By avoiding **these common mistakes,** you can ensure that your name recognition training is as efficient and enjoyable as possible.

**It's all about building a positive connection between you and your puppy,** and their name plays a significant role in that.

Happy training!

*Photo by **Harrison Kugler** on **Unsplash***

# 6. MAINTAINING AND REINFORCING NAME RECOGNITION

**You did it!** Your puppy now responds to their name. But, **remember**, this isn't where your journey ends.

Just like any learned skill, name recognition **needs to be maintained and reinforced**.

Here's how you can ensure that your puppy's name continues to be a **powerful tool** for their attention:

## 1. Consistent Use of Their Name

**Consistency is key** in dog training, and name recognition is no exception. Continue to use your puppy's name regularly to keep it fresh in their mind. However, remember our note from the common mistakes section: **avoid overuse. It's a balance.**

## 2. Positive Reinforcement

Even after your puppy is responding consistently to their name, continue to reward them sporadically. This doesn't have to be a treat every time - **a pat, praise, or a quick game can also serve as a reward**. This reinforces the positive association with their name.

### 3. Use Their Name in Different Contexts

Don't limit using your puppy's name for training sessions only. **Integrate it into daily activities**. Call them by their name when it's mealtime, playtime, or when you just want to give them a cuddle.

This helps solidify their understanding that their name is a direct call to them, **not just a command for attention**.

### 4. Practice in Various Environments

Your home isn't the only place your pup needs to respond to their name. Practice name recognition in different environments, **from calm to distracting ones**.

This will help your puppy **learn to respond** to their name no matter where they are or what's going on around them.

### 5. Regularly Test Name Recognition

**Occasionally**, throughout your day, call your puppy's name **when they're not expecting it**. This helps maintain their alertness to their name and provides you with a chance to praise and reward them for their quick response.

**Remember**, training doesn't stop once your puppy learns a skill; it's an ongoing process.

Keep training sessions **short, positive, and fun**.

Your puppy's name is a simple word that plays a significant role in your communication with them, **so keep it special**.

You've got this! **Bravo to you both!**

*Photo by **Ayla Verschueren** on Unsplash*

# HOUSEBREAKING/ POTTY TRAINING

### Introduction

One of the **most essential training elements** for any new puppy is housebreaking, or potty training.

This skill is not only vital for maintaining a clean and odor-free home, but it also helps to **establish a sense of routine and order** for your puppy, contributing to their overall sense of security and well-being.

Teaching your puppy where and when they should do their business **may seem daunting at first**, especially with the inevitable accidents along the way. However, with the right approach, **plenty of patience, and a consistent routine**, your puppy will eventually get the hang of it.

As with any form of training, it's important to remember that **every puppy is different**.

Some may pick up on housebreaking cues quickly, while others may need a little more time and patience. What's most important is to **maintain a positive attitude and make the**

**process as stress-free as possible** for your furry friend.

**Remember**, it's not about perfection; it's about progress.

In the following sections, we'll break down the step-by-step process of housebreaking, discuss how to handle accidents, and provide tips for making the training process smooth and effective.

So, let's start this journey with a positive mindset and remember, **you're not alone in this**.

Thousands of puppy parents have successfully housebroken their puppies, **and so will you!**

# 1. THE IMPORTANCE OF HOUSEBREAKING/ POTTY TRAINING

Housebreaking, or potty training, is a critical part of integrating a new puppy into your household.

It's **among the first things you'll want to teach** your new furry friend, and it's not just about keeping your floors clean (though that's a definite plus!).

Let's dive into **why housebreaking is so important**.

First and foremost, housebreaking is about instilling **healthy habits in your puppy. Just as children** need to learn to use the bathroom properly, so do puppies. It's part of their journey from carefree young pups into well-behaved adult dogs.

It's not just about convenience for you as an owner (though we'll admit, life is easier when you're not constantly cleaning up messes); it's also a **fundamental aspect of your puppy's development and growth**.

**Moreover**, housebreaking your puppy is a **matter of hygiene and health**, for both you and your puppy. The cleaner and more sanitary your living environment, the less likely it is that either of you will encounter **harmful bacteria or parasites**. Also, a well-potty-trained dog is less likely to have accidents that could potentially cause injury, like slipping on a wet floor.

Consistent housebreaking training can also **strengthen your bond** with your puppy.

**Remember**, training of any sort is an interaction between you and your pet, a shared task **that requires communication and cooperation**.

It offers a chance for you to spend quality time together, understand each other better, and to establish a relationship based on trust and mutual respect. When your dog understands what you want from them and gets it right, it can **boost their confidence**, making them happier and even more eager to please.

In addition, **effective housebreaking can reduce stress for both you and your pet**.

Knowing exactly when and where they're supposed to 'go' **gives your dog a sense of security**. And for you, there's the relief of not having to worry about coming home to a mess or facing embarrassment when guests visit.

Lastly, a **well housebroken dog is easier to care for in multiple contexts**. For example, if your dog ever needs to be boarded, or if you want to travel with your pet, having a dog that's reliable in its bathroom habits makes everything much smoother.

In conclusion, the process of housebreaking or **potty training is a crucial step in your journey with your new puppy**. Not only does it create a cleaner and more harmonious living environment, but it also **strengthens the bond** between you and your puppy, and paves the way for further training and shared adventures.

It requires patience and consistency, but **the payoff is well worth the effort**.

So, let's get started!

# 2. PREPARING FOR HOUSEBREAKING: NECESSARY SUPPLIES

The journey of housebreaking is about to begin, and you know what they say: a good workman never blames their tools. **Being well-prepared with the right supplies** can make this task smoother and more successful.

Let's explore what you'll need for this venture.

### a. *A Quality Crate*

A crate is more than just a place for your puppy to sleep. **It's a fundamental tool for housebreaking**. Dogs naturally avoid soiling their sleeping area, making a crate an effective means to control their toilet habits. **Choose a crate** that's just large enough for your puppy to stand up, turn around, and lie down in. It should be cozy, not cavernous, to discourage your pup from using one corner as a bathroom.

### b. *Leashes and Harnesses*

A leash will be your guiding hand during potty training. It allows you to direct your puppy to the desired bathroom spot and keeps them from wandering off. A harness can be used for smaller puppies or breeds, providing control **without putting pressure on their necks**.

### c. *Puppy Pads*

Sometimes, outdoor training isn't feasible - whether due to your puppy's vaccination schedule, living situation, or inclement weather. **In these cases**, puppy pads are handy. They're absorbent, waterproof-backed mats that can be placed around your home to provide an indoor bathroom spot. Some are scented to attract puppies to use them.

### d.      *Pet-friendly Cleaning Supplies*

**Accidents will happen**, and it's important to clean up thoroughly. Dog urine contains pheromones that can attract your puppy back to the same spot. Use a **pet-friendly enzymatic cleaner** that breaks down these **pheromones** to avoid repeat offenses. Regular household cleaners may not effectively eliminate these scent markers.

### e.      *Treats*

**Positive reinforcement is crucial** in any training, and housebreaking is no exception. Rewarding your puppy with a small treat immediately after they 'do their business' in the right spot can work wonders. Choose treats that are small, easy to digest, and something your puppy finds irresistible.

### f.      *Patience and Consistency*

Okay, so these aren't supplies you can buy, but they're crucial ingredients for successful housebreaking. **Remember**, your puppy is just learning the ropes, and accidents are part of the process. **Stay patient, be consistent** with your routine, and celebrate the small victories. **You'll get there**!

**Remember**, the goal of housebreaking is not just about teaching your puppy where to go potty but also about **instilling a routine** and a sense of responsibility in them. Having these supplies at hand will enable you **to start on the right paw**, making the process more enjoyable and less stressful for both you and your new furry friend.

Let's embark on this potty training journey with optimism, preparedness, and the right tools!

# 3. UNDERSTANDING PUPPY'S BATHROOM HABITS

Before we dive headfirst into the training process, it's vital to get a grasp of your puppy's bathroom habits.

Just like us humans, dogs too have their own rhythms and routines. **Knowing what to expect** can significantly aid your housebreaking journey.

So, let's get down to the basics.

## 1. Frequent Needs

Puppies are a lot like infants - **small bladders, limited control**, and frequent bathroom needs. A general rule of thumb is that a juvenile dog, a poppy, can hold their bladder for **as many hours as they are months old, plus one. For instance, a two-month-old puppy might need a bathroom break every three hours.**

## 2. After Activity Bathroom Breaks

Always **remember** - eat, play, pee, repeat! Puppies typically need to go to the bathroom after they wake up from a nap, after meals, and after play sessions. It's all that excitement and movement that gets things going, so **be prepared for a bathroom break following these activities**.

## 3. Nighttime Needs

Younger puppies **might need one or two bathroom breaks during the night**. If your puppy wakes up and is restless, it's likely they need to go. As they grow older, they will eventually be able to hold it through the night.

## 4. Whining, Circling, Sniffing

These are telltale signs your pup needs to go. If you notice your puppy suddenly start sniffing the floor intently, whining, or circling, **it's time for a bathroom break**. These signs will become more apparent as you get to know your pup better.

## 5. Consistent Spot

**Dogs are creatures of habit.** Once they've picked a spot where they like to do their business, they will usually stick to it. This will work to your advantage during housebreaking.

**Remember**, the key to successful housebreaking is patience and observation.

Keep a close eye on your puppy, **learn their signals**, and provide them with ample opportunities to go to the bathroom in the right place.

By **understanding** your puppy's bathroom habits, you can **anticipate their needs** setting them up for success, making housebreaking a smoother and more enjoyable experience for both of you.

**Trust in the process, and believe in your puppy** - they are learning something entirely new, and with your guidance and support, they will surely get the hang of it!

# 4. SETTING UP A ROUTINE FOR HOUSEBREAKING

Establishing a **consistent routine is pivotal to successful housebreaking**. Dogs, like humans, thrive on routine.

**A predictable schedule helps your puppy** understand when it's time to eat, play, and most importantly, do their business.

Let's explore how to structure an effective routine for housebreaking your puppy.

### 1.                  *Feeding Schedule*

Regulated feeding times can lead to predictable bathroom times. Depending on their age, **puppies should be fed three to four times a day**. Your vet can help you determine the optimal feeding schedule. **Avoid free-feeding** (leaving food out all day), as it makes bathroom habits less predictable.

### 2.                  *Potty Breaks*

Plan regular bathroom breaks. Remember, a puppy can generally hold their bladder for **their age in months plus one hour**. This means a three-month-old puppy will need a break every four hours at least. However, **more frequent breaks are better in the beginning.**

### 3.                  *Activity Times*

Regular play and exercise sessions are not only vital for your puppy's physical development but **also help to tire them out**, leading to fewer behaviour issues. Additionally, **remember** that puppies often need a bathroom break after physical activity.

### 4.                  *Sleep Times*

A bedtime routine helps your puppy understand when it's

time to settle down. Remember, **younger puppies may still need nighttime bathroom breaks**.

## 5.  *Alone Times*

It's essential for your puppy to become comfortable with being alone to prevent separation anxiety. Begin by leaving them alone **for short periods** and gradually increase the time as they grow older.

**Here's a sample routine for a three-month-old puppy**:

7:00 AM: Wake up and immediately go out for a potty break.

7:30 AM: Feed breakfast followed by a bathroom break.

8:00 AM: Playtime followed by a bathroom break.

9:00 AM: Naptime.

12:00 PM: Wake up, go out for a potty break, feed lunch followed by a bathroom break.

12:30 PM: Playtime followed by a bathroom break.

1:30 PM: Naptime.

4:00 PM: Wake up, go out for a potty break.

5:30 PM: Feed dinner followed by a bathroom break.

6:00 PM: Playtime followed by a bathroom break.

8:00 PM: Last call for water.

9:00 PM: Final play session and bathroom break.

10:00 PM: Final potty break before bedtime.

**Remember**, the goal here is **consistency**.

Yes, accidents will happen, but by maintaining a routine, you'll be setting your puppy up for success.

In the words of Benjamin Franklin, "**By failing to prepare, you are preparing to fail**".

So let's start preparing for success!

# 5. INDOOR VS OUTDOOR POTTY TRAINING: WHICH TO CHOOSE?

Ah, the classic indoor vs outdoor potty training debate! It can be a real head-scratcher for many new dog parents.

**But don't worry**, we're here to help you make an informed decision.

Let's break down the pros and cons of these two methods so that you can choose the one that's best **suited for your lifestyle and your pup's needs**.

## *Outdoor Potty Training*

**The traditional approach**, outdoor potty training has its own set of advantages and disadvantages.

**Pros**

1. **Natural Environment**

Dogs instinctively **prefer to eliminate outside**, making this a natural choice.

2. **Healthier**

Less risk of bacteria or parasites in your home.

3. **No Need for Transition**

If your puppy is trained to go outside from the start, you don't need to transition them later.

**Cons**

1. **Requires Frequent Access to Outside**

You need to be able to get your pup outside quickly when they need to go, which can be tricky if you live in an apartment or work away from home.

2. **Weather Dependent**

Bad weather can complicate potty breaks.

## *Indoor Potty Training*

Indoor potty training can be a great alternative for those who can't frequently take their pup outside.

**Pros**

### 1. Convenience

Indoor potty training can be a lifesaver for apartment dwellers, those with limited mobility, or anyone who can't frequently take their pup outside.

### 2. Weather Independent

No need to worry about the elements interrupting your puppy's potty routine.

### 3. Good for Small or Toy Breeds

Smaller breeds often struggle with the cold, making indoor training a more comfortable option for them.

**Cons**

### 1. Potential for Confusion

It can be harder for puppies to understand that they can only go in specific indoor spots, not just anywhere inside.

### 2. Transition to Outside May Be Needed

If you ever want your dog to switch to going outside, you'll need to retrain them, which can be challenging.

**Remember**, your choice between indoor and outdoor potty training should be based on what's best for both your puppy and your lifestyle.

Don't let anyone else **pressure you** into a choice that doesn't suit your circumstances.

Your **dog will adapt to either method** with your consistent guidance and support. After all, dogs are about the most adaptable creatures on earth!

So, **take a deep breath**, make your choice confidently, and let's move forward in this housebreaking journey!

# 6. STEP-BY-STEP GUIDE TO HOUSEBREAKING/ POTTY TRAINING

Alright, it's time to roll up your sleeves and start the housebreaking process! This might feel daunting, but remember, **every dog owner has gone through this**.

**You're not alone**, and with consistency, patience, and the following steps, you'll be able to navigate this phase successfully.

Let's dive right in!

**Step-by-Step**

## Step 1: Establish a Routine

**Dogs thrive on routine**. Feed your puppy at the same times each day and take them out to potty on a consistent schedule.

Typically, puppies need to relieve themselves after waking up, eating, playing, and before bed. **Young puppies might need to go out every hour or two.**

## Step 2: Choose the 'Bathroom Spot'

Choose a **specific spot** outdoors (or a particular place indoors if you're indoor training). Always take your puppy to this spot when it's time to go. This **helps** your pup associate that location with going to the bathroom.

## Step 3: Use a Cue Word or Phrase

As your puppy starts to go, softly **say a cue word or phrase like "Go Potty."** With time, your puppy will associate the phrase with the act of elimination, which can make bathroom breaks more efficient.

## Step 4: Praise and Reward

Once your pup does their business, **praise them in a cheerful voice** and offer a treat. This positive reinforcement makes your puppy more likely to repeat the behaviour.

### Step 5: Supervise Indoors

When inside, **keep a close eye on your puppy to catch signs they need to go**, like sniffing around or circling. If you notice these signs, quickly but calmly take them out to their spot.

### Step 6: Confine When You Can't Supervise

If you can't actively supervise your puppy (like if you're cooking or need to leave the house), confine them in a **puppy-proof area or crate**.

**Remember**, confinement isn't a punishment; it's a tool to prevent accidents and keep your puppy safe.

### Step 7: Handle Accidents Calmly

**Accidents will happen**. When they do, **remain calm. Don't punish your puppy** as this can create fear and confusion. Instead, quietly clean up with an **enzymatic cleaner** to remove any odours that could attract them back to the spot.

### Step 8: Gradually Increase Freedom

As your pup becomes more reliable, gradually give them more freedom to roam in your home. This should be a **slow process** over weeks or even months.

**Remember**, potty training is a marathon, not a sprint. **It takes time and patience**.

But, with **consistency** and following these steps, you're setting your pup - and yourself - up for success.

So, keep the faith and remember: **you've got this!**

# 7. NIGHTTIME HOUSEBREAKING TIPS

Just as the moon takes over the sky at night, a new set of challenges might take over your housebreaking routine.

**Nighttime housebreaking** can be a real test of patience, but with the right strategies, it can be smoothly navigated.

So, let's look at how we can turn these night-owl necessities into a dreamy routine.

### 1. *Limit Water Before Bed*

It's a good practice to limit your puppy's water intake around 2 hours before their bedtime. Of course, **make sure** your puppy is well hydrated throughout the day. If they're thirsty, **don't deny them water**, but try to ensure they're getting enough to drink earlier in the evening.

### 2. *Last Call for Potty*

Just before it's time to turn off the lights, take your pup out for one last bathroom break. **Make sure they do their business**, praising them when they do.

This last call can help them stay comfortable throughout the night.

### 3. *Cozy Crate*

Crate training can be a big help during the night. Dogs **naturally** avoid soiling their sleeping area, so a crate encourages them to hold it.

The **crate should be comfortable**, with a soft bed, and just large enough for them to stand up, turn around, and lie down. **It's their cozy den, not a cage**.

### 4. *Respond to Potty Cries*

In the early weeks, your puppy may need a **nighttime bathroom break**. If they cry in the night and you suspect it's for a potty run, respond quickly. Carry them to the potty spot, and **remember** to keep this an all-business trip. No playtime or treats—just a quick in-and-out.

## 5.      Keep Your Cool During Accidents

If an accident happens, **remember to stay calm**. It's frustrating, but it's also a part of the process. Clean it up with an **enzymatic** cleaner and continue with your routine.

## 6.      Gradual Progression

As your pup gets older, they'll be able to hold it longer. This **progress will be gradual** but celebrate it. Soon, your puppy will be sleeping through the night without any need for a bathroom break.

Nighttime housebreaking doesn't have to be a nightmare. With **patience, consistency**, and these tips, you'll help your puppy master this skill.

**Remember**, every small success is a step towards a fully housebroken pup.

**So keep going; you're doing great!**

# 8. DEALING WITH ACCIDENTS: CLEAN-UP AND PREVENTION

Hey there, master dog trainer!

I can see you've come a long way in your housebreaking journey with your pup. **Accidents**, though frustrating, are **just little speed bumps** on this journey.

**They're as natural as they are inevitable**.

In this section, we'll focus on how to handle these messy mishaps, clean them effectively, and, most importantly, **prevent them** from happening again.

## *Cleaning Up the Accident*

Let's start by saying this: catching your dog "in the act" is rare, and it's more likely you'll find a surprise waiting for you. **But don't worry!** Cleaning it up is simple.

**For urine**: Soak up as much as possible of the urine using paper towels or an absorbent cloth. After the spot is mostly dry, **use an enzymatic cleaner** specifically made for pet accidents. These cleaners break down the **urine's proteins**, eliminating the odour and reducing the likelihood your dog will be drawn to the same spot.

**For feces**: Pick up as much as possible using a bag or gloves. Dispose of it properly and clean the area **with the enzymatic cleaner.**

**Never use cleaners containing ammonia** for accidents, as they can mimic the smell of urine and draw your pup back to the same spot.

## *Preventing Future Accidents*

Accidents can be disheartening, but they're also learning opportunities. Here are **some tips** to prevent future accidents:

### A. Maintain a Regular Schedule

Regular feeding times lead to predictable bathroom times.

### B. Frequent Potty Breaks

Puppies have small bladders and need frequent breaks.

### C. Watch for Signals

Learn to read your dog's potty signals. These may include pacing, sniffing, or circling.

### D. Limit Space

Until your pup is fully house-trained, limit their access to the whole house. Use baby gates or playpens to confine them to a smaller area.

**Positive Reinforcement**: Celebrate every successful outdoor bathroom trip with praise, petting, or a small treat.

**Remember**, every dog learns **at their own pace**.

Your patience, understanding, and consistency are the keys to their successful housebreaking. Believe in your training abilities, trust in your pup's potential, and keep moving forward. **You've got this!**

# 9. COMMON MISTAKES AND HOW TO AVOID THEM

Hello, patient trainers! As we navigate this potty training journey, it's important to **remember that everyone makes mistakes** – and that includes both you and your pup!

Mistakes are often our **most valuable teachers**.

Let's explore some of the common mistakes made during housebreaking and, most importantly, how to avoid them.

## 1. Expecting Instant Results

The first mistake is expecting your pup to master housebreaking overnight. Potty training is a process that **takes time**, consistency, and a whole lot of patience.

**Remember**, your puppy is **just a baby learning about the world**.

**How to Avoid**: Understand that housebreaking is a journey with ups and downs. Celebrate small victories and stay patient with setbacks.

## 2. Inconsistent Routine

Puppies thrive on routine. An inconsistent feeding or potty schedule can confuse your puppy and **lead to accidents**.

**How to Avoid**: Establish and stick to a consistent routine. **Regular** feeding times lead to predictable potty times.

## 3. Negative Reinforcement

Reacting negatively or punishing your pup for an accident can **create fear and confusion**, making the training process **longer and more difficult**.

**How to Avoid**: Use **positive reinforcement** for successful outdoor bathroom trips. If an accident happens, stay calm, clean it up, **and move on.**

### 4. Cleaning Mistakes

Not cleaning up thoroughly after accidents can **leave lingering smells** that attract your pup back to the same spot.

**How to Avoid**: Always clean accidents with an **enzymatic cleaner** to fully break down the smell. Remember, **never use ammonia**-based cleaners.

### 5. Ignoring Potty Signals

Each pup will have its way of indicating they need to go out. Ignoring these signals can lead to accidents.

**How to Avoid**: Learn your pup's **unique signals**, which might include sniffing, circling, or pacing. Respond promptly when you notice these signs.

### 6. Giving Too Much Freedom Too Soon

Allowing your puppy to roam free in the house before they're fully housebroken can lead to accidents **in hidden spots**.

**How to Avoid**: Limit your pup's space until they're fully housebroken. Use gates or pens to confine them to an area where you can keep an eye on them.

**Remember**, every mistake is a learning opportunity for both of you.

Continue to train with **love, patience, and positivity**.

**You and your furry friend are doing great, keep going!**

# 10. PROGRESS AND PATIENCE: UNDERSTANDING THE TRAINING TIMELINE

**Hey there, champion trainers!**

As we continue this exciting journey, one critical concept you must remember is this: **Patience is your most powerful tool**. Training is a process, and as with any worthwhile endeavour, it will take time.

In this chapter, we'll explore the training timeline to help manage your expectations and **maintain your enthusiasm**.

## *Understanding Your Pup's Development*

To begin with, let's **remember** that puppies are **like small children**; they are still learning and growing. A **puppy's bladder is tiny**, and their control over it will increase gradually as they mature.

**At 8 weeks old, a pup may need to go outside every 30 to 60 minutes**. By 16 weeks, they might hold it for 2 hours, and by 6 months, they could last up to 4-6 hours during the day.

Just like with children, **each pup is unique**, and progress may vary. Some pups may take longer than others to fully grasp potty training concepts, **and that's perfectly okay**.

## *Setting Realistic Expectations*

Puppies, depending on their age, size, and breed, may take anywhere **from a few weeks to a few months** to become fully housebroken. It's crucial to **set realistic expectations** and remember that there will be progress and setbacks along the way.

A key point to remember: **Accidents don't mean failure**. It's all part of the journey. A setback is not a step back; it's just another opportunity for learning and growth.

## Maintaining Patience and Positivity

**Patience and positivity** are your guiding lights throughout this process.

Puppies pick up on your emotions. **They know when you're frustrated**, which can **make them anxious** and potentially slow the training process. So, even when it feels challenging, always approach training with **a calm, positive demeanour**.

## Consistent Reinforcement

Keep in mind, **consistency is key**.

The more consistent you are with your routine and rewards, the faster your pup will learn. Even after your pup seems to have mastered potty training, **keep reinforcing good behaviour** for several weeks. This will help solidify their learning and make their potty habits second nature.

At the end of the day, remember this: **every pup is unique, every journey is different, and every moment is a chance to bond.**

So hold onto your patience, **stay positive**, and relish this unique experience. You're not just training your puppy; you're building a lifelong friendship.

So let's keep going—**you and your pup are doing an amazing job!**

# 11. REINFORCING HOUSEBREAKING: ONGOING TRAINING

**Hello again, superb puppy trainers!** As we continue this amazing journey together, let's delve into the world of reinforcement training.

**Remember**, housebreaking is not a one-and-done deal—it's a process that continues long after your pup has gotten the hang of it. But don't worry; it's **not as daunting as it may sound**.

With the right knowledge and a positive attitude, you can navigate this stage like the excellent trainers you are!

## Consistency is Key

**The first rule of reinforcement is consistency**. Once your pup has gotten a good grasp of housebreaking, it's crucial to **maintain the routines** you've established. This means keeping to regular feeding, play, and potty times.

Puppies thrive on routine; it **helps them understand** what is expected and when.

## Reward, Reward, Reward

Rewarding your puppy for good behaviour is still a vital part of the process. By now, your little buddy is used to getting a tasty treat or an excited **"good job!"** whenever they do their business outside.

**Don't stop that** just because they've gotten good at it. This ongoing reward system will help **ensure that their good habits stick**.

## Watch for Signals

Even well-trained puppies might **occasionally have**

**accidents**, especially when they're excited or nervous. But as you continue to reinforce their training, they'll start to give signals when they need to go. It could be **a certain look, a specific bark, or a move toward the door**.

Recognizing and responding to these signals promptly can help **solidify their training**.

## Patience and Positivity

As I've said before, **patience and positivity** are your best friends in this journey. Puppies are smart, and they're sensitive to your moods. Maintaining a **positive attitude**, even when there are little accidents, will help your pup stay confident and eager to learn.

## Maintenance and Adaptation

As your puppy grows, so will their bladder control, and you may need to **adjust your routine accordingly**. The schedule that worked for a 3-month-old puppy might not suit a 9-month-old.

**Stay attuned to your pup's needs and adapt** as required.

**The road to a fully housebroken pup is a journey, not a sprint**.

There will be plenty of laughter, a few messy clean-ups, and countless memorable moments along the way. But **remember**, every step you take is bringing you closer to a well-trained, confident dog who's as proud of their progress as you are.

So, ready to conquer the world of ongoing housebreaking reinforcement?

**Let's get to it, champion trainers!**

# 12. RESOURCES AND FURTHER READING

Well done, esteemed trainers!

You've journeyed with me through the challenging, but rewarding, process **of housebreaking your puppy**.

We've been through the nitty-gritty details, common mistakes, tips, and everything in between. However, remember that learning never ends, and the best trainers are lifelong learners.

Should you want to delve deeper, there are a multitude of resources available on the internet to enrich your knowledge. Some are web-based, others are engaging videos.

**Remember** one of our other books, *"Puppy Training 101: A Practical Guide for Young Dog Owners?"* It's a resource to return to time and again, as your pup grows and your training journey progresses.

There's always something more to learn, **something more to revisit**.

**Embrace the journey,** my fantastic trainers, because this is more than just training—it's about **building an everlasting bond with your furry friend**.

**Remember**, even the smallest progress is progress nonetheless. As long as you keep going, keep learning, and keep loving, you and your pup will grow together in this wonderful adventure.

So, let's keep moving forward!

The world of puppy training is yours to master, and I'm right here, **cheering you on every step of the way.**

I also strongly suggest to read Decoding Dog Speak: Dog-Human Dialogues and the AI Frontier: Exploring Dog-Human

Dialogue and AI's Future Role

Embark on an eye-opening journey into the fascinating world of dog-human dialogue with this specific book.

Discover the rich history of our canine companions, dive deep into the intricate world of canine communication with this meticulously researched guide, uncovering how dogs express themselves to humans and how advancements, including AI technologies, can redefine our relationship with our four-legged companions.

*Photo by **charlesdeluvio** on **Unsplash***

# BEHAVIOURAL ISSUES

## Introduction

**Welcome to a new, critical chapter** in your journey with your furry friend!

It's time to tackle the various behavioural issues that could arise with a puppy. **No journey is ever entirely smooth**, and it's quite the same with raising a puppy.

**But fear not!**

As we've learned together in this book, every bump along the way is another **opportunity for growth and understanding—** for both you and your puppy.

When we talk about "**behavioural issues**," we refer to **certain actions or habits** that your puppy may develop, which could be **problematic, bothersome, or even harmful**.

These include but are not limited to: chewing on furniture or shoes, excessive barking, biting, or showing signs of separation anxiety. **These behaviours are normal to an extent**—it's part of being a puppy, after all.

However, **if left unchecked, these behaviours can escalate**, creating an unhealthy environment for you, your family, and your puppy.

It's important to **remember** that behavioural issues **don't mean** your puppy is "bad."

They're merely exhibiting behaviours that **are instinctual or reactive** to their environment or circumstances. It's up to us, as responsible and loving pet parents, **to guide them towards better habits.**

**Remember** our goal here: to foster a happy, healthy relationship with your puppy, ensuring they grow into a well-adjusted adult dog.

In this section, we're going to explore the **most common behavioural issues** you may encounter and understand why puppies may develop these habits. **With understanding comes empathy, and with empathy comes patience**—the key ingredients to successful training.

We'll then delve into **tried and true techniques** for addressing these issues, using positive reinforcement methods that keep your puppy's welfare at heart. Remember, **punishment is not our path**. We want to **encourage good behaviour**, not instill fear.

This approach creates a **stronger bond** between you and your puppy, **a bond based on trust and mutual respect.**

Lastly, we'll look at **preventive measures** to stop these issues from becoming persistent habits, and how to determine when it might be necessary to seek professional help.

This journey may be challenging, **but it's nothing we can't tackle together**. Just imagine the sense of achievement when you and your puppy overcome these hurdles.

It's all part of the **adventure** that makes having a puppy so rewarding!

So, let's jump right in, shall we?

We've got this!

# 1. COMMON PUPPY BEHAVIORAL ISSUES

Navigating through the journey of puppyhood can sometimes feel like charting a course through unknown waters. A vast sea of **unexpected behaviours** awaits you, **but rest assured, you're not alone**, and your trusty map—that's this book!—is right here to guide you.

Let's dive into some of the most common behavioural issues that you might encounter with your puppy.

Remember, **having issues doesn't mean your puppy is problematic**. It just means they're **learning and exploring their boundaries**, and it's up to us to guide them in the right direction.

## Biting and Nipping

It's **entirely natural** for puppies to bite or nip during play or when they're teething. It's a part of their exploration of the world around them. **However**, it's crucial to teach them to control this behaviour to avoid accidental injuries as they grow and their jaws become stronger.

## Excessive Barking

Puppies bark for various reasons: excitement, boredom, anxiety, or to get your attention. While **some barking is normal**, excessive barking can become a problem if it disturbs you, your family, or neighbours.

## Chewing

Chewing is another **common behaviour** for puppies, especially when they're teething. While it's a natural behaviour, they need to learn what is acceptable to chew (like their toys) and what isn't (**like your shoes**).

## Separation Anxiety

Some puppies may find it **difficult to be alone**, leading to separation anxiety. This behaviour can manifest in several ways, such as excessive barking, chewing, or even house-soiling when you're away.

## Jumping Up

While it can be cute when your little puppy jumps up to greet you, this behaviour can become a problem as your puppy grows into an adult dog. It's best to **teach them polite greetings** from an early age.

## House Soiling

House soiling or potty training accidents are a typical part of puppyhood. **Patience, consistency, and a good cleaning routine** are key in overcoming this challenge.

Each of these behaviours, while common, **can be managed and improved** with the right training approach, patience, and consistency.

**Remember**, your puppy isn't acting out to defy you—they're learning and need your guidance.

In the coming sections, **we'll discuss how to address these issues in a positive, effective way.**

So, buckle up and get ready to navigate these waters with confidence and positivity!

**You've got this!**

# 2. UNDERSTANDING WHY PUPPIES MISBEHAVE

As we step into the enchanting world of puppyhood, we might be taken aback by their behaviours that we interpret as 'misbehaving.'

From chewing your favourite shoes to barking at the wind, puppy behaviours can be both endearing and baffling!

But it's crucial to **remember** that puppies aren't tiny humans; **they're a different species with their own set of instincts and ways of understanding the world.**

## *Puppy Exploration*

Puppies **use their mouth as we use our hands**. They explore their world by nibbling, chewing, and tasting. This can lead to biting, chewing on furniture, or even gobbling up something harmful.

It's **crucial to provide safe and appropriate chew toys** satisfying their urge to chew and keep them away from harmful objects.

## *Communication*

Puppies bark, whine, or growl **to communicate their needs, fears, or excitement**. However, some puppies may resort to excessive barking or growling if they feel misunderstood or if they've learned that these behaviours get them attention.

## *Boundless Energy*

Puppies are bursting with energy and need plenty of physical and mental stimulation. Not enough exercise and boredom can lead to destructive behaviours like chewing, digging, or excessive barking. **Regular exercise and mental stimulation through training or puzzle toys** can help channel this energy constructively.

## Separation Anxiety

**Puppies are social creatures** and can find it hard to be alone. This can lead to behaviours like constant whining, barking, or destruction when left alone. **Gradually** teaching them to be comfortable when alone can help overcome this issue.

## Testing Boundaries

Just like human children, puppies test boundaries to understand the world around them and learn what's acceptable behaviour. This can sometimes be perceived as 'misbehaving' or 'defiance,' but **it's a part of their learning process**.

## Lack of Training

Often, behaviours we interpret as 'misbehaving' are just **untrained behaviours**. **Remember**, puppies don't arrive knowing human rules. **It's up to us to teach them in a gentle, positive way**.

**Understanding** why puppies 'misbehave' is the first step in effectively addressing behavioural issues. It allows us to empathize with our puppies and approach their training with kindness and patience.

In the next sections, we'll delve into **specific strategies to manage common puppy behaviours**, armed with the knowledge of why they occur.

Let's turn these behavioural challenges into training triumphs together!

# 3. SOLUTIONS AND TECHNIQUES FOR ADDRESSING BEHAVIORAL ISSUES

Puppies, with their boundless energy and curiosity, can certainly keep us on our toes!

It's vital to **remember**, though, that their 'misbehaviours' aren't personal. Puppies aren't being naughty or trying to test us - **they are simply learning and trying to understand their world.**

**As their guides**, we can channel their energy and curiosity into positive behaviours using these solutions and techniques:

## Positive Reinforcement

Always **remember** that positive reinforcement is the most powerful tool in your training kit. Rewarding your puppy for good behaviour will **motivate** them to repeat it. Treats, praise, toys, or a quick game can all be used as rewards.

## Redirecting Behavior

If your puppy is engaging in a behaviour you don't want, like chewing on a shoe, try **redirecting their attention** to something acceptable, like a chew toy. Over time, your puppy will learn what items are acceptable to chew on.

## Training Sessions

Regular, **short training sessions** can work wonders. Use these sessions to teach basic commands and manners. **Remember** to keep the training positive and fun!

## Exercise and Mental Stimulation

Ensure your puppy has enough physical exercise and mental stimulation every day. Boredom and excess energy can often lead to destructive behaviours. Long walks, playtimes, puzzle toys, and interactive games can keep your puppy **content and tired**.

## Socialization

Expose your puppy to a variety of people, places, and situations to help them grow into a well-adjusted adult dog. **Positive early experiences** can prevent many behavioural problems, like fear and aggression.

## Consistent Rules

Dogs thrive on consistency. Make sure **all family members** follow the **same rules** and use the **same commands**. It can be confusing for your puppy if they are allowed to do something one day and then scolded for it the next.

## Patience and Understanding

Puppies are learning and **will make mistakes**. It's essential to be patient and never resort to punishment, which can be harmful and ineffective.

These techniques provide a foundation for addressing behavioural issues.

In the following sections, **we'll look at specific strategies** for common problems like biting, chewing, and barking.

**Remember**, every puppy is unique and may learn at their own pace.

**Training is a journey, not a destination**, and each step your puppy takes towards good behaviour is a victory to celebrate.

Let's embark on this journey together with **positivity, patience, and persistence!**

# 4. PREVENTING BEHAVIORAL ISSUES

Prevention, as they say, is always better than cure.

In the world of puppy training, this means **shaping positive behaviours from the get-go and providing an environment that allows your puppy to thrive**.

By doing so, you can potentially prevent many behavioural issues from developing.

**Here's how**.

## Start Training Early

Begin training your puppy **as soon as they arrive home**. Puppies are learning machines, and the earlier you start, the better. **Remember**, you're not just training commands; you're instilling good manners and habits, **setting the foundation** for a well-behaved adult dog.

## Establish a Routine

Dogs love predictability. Set up a **daily routine** for meals, potty breaks, training sessions, playtime, and bedtime. A stable routine helps your puppy **feel secure** and can prevent anxiety-related issues.

## Socialize Your Puppy

Early and positive exposure to a variety of people, animals, places, and experiences can help prevent behavioural issues such as **fear, aggression, and anxiety**. Take your puppy to different environments, invite friends over, introduce them to well-behaved adult dogs - all under **controlled, positive circumstances**.

## Provide Plenty of Exercise and Mental Stimulation

Many behavioural issues, such as excessive chewing and barking, stem from boredom or excess energy. Make sure your puppy gets lots of **physical exercise and mental stimulation** through play, training, walks, and dog-appropriate puzzle toys.

## Be Consistent

Consistency is key in preventing behavioural issues. Ensure **all family members** follow the same rules and use the same commands to **avoid confusing your puppy**.

## Use Positive Reinforcement:

Always reward desired behaviour. Puppies are more likely to repeat actions that result in positive outcomes. **Ignore undesirable behaviour** and reward the good, and you'll shape your puppy's behaviour in a positive way.

## Monitor Your Puppy's Health

Many behavioural issues can stem from **underlying health problems**. Regular vet check-ups and keeping an eye on your puppy's health **can prevent these issues**.

**Remember, you are your puppy's guide, teacher, and protector.**

With your steady hand and caring heart, you can guide them away from behavioural pitfalls and towards positive habits.

The work you do now in **preventing behavioural issues will pay dividends in the future**, fostering a harmonious and joyful relationship between you and your puppy.

**Let's embrace this challenge**, knowing that every effort made is a step towards a happier, healthier life for our beloved canine companions.

# 5. WHEN TO SEEK PROFESSIONAL HELP

Training a puppy is a journey, one that is rewarding, but can sometimes be challenging.

Despite our best efforts, there may be times when a puppy's behavioural **issues persist or escalate**, leading to moments of uncertainty and frustration.

This is completely normal, and in these instances, it's crucial to understand when and how to **seek professional help**.

**Signs That It's Time to Consult a Professional**

### *Persistent, Unmanageable Behaviors*

If your puppy continues to exhibit problematic behaviours despite your consistent and dedicated training efforts, it may be **time to consult** a professional.

### *Escalating Aggression*

If your puppy displays signs of growing aggression—such as snapping, growling, or biting—**it's crucial to seek help immediately**. These behaviours **can become dangerous** if left unaddressed.

### *Severe Anxiety or Fear*

Some dogs may exhibit extreme fear or anxiety, manifested through constant shaking, hiding, or even aggressive behaviour. **Professional guidance** can help address these issues effectively.

### *Sudden Change in Behavior*

A sudden change in your puppy's behaviour, such as a loss of appetite, sudden aggression, or excessive whining, can be a sign of an **underlying medical issue**. In this case, consult your vet first.

**Choosing the Right Professional**

The world of dog training can be confusing, with various titles like **behaviourists, trainers, and consultants.**

Here's a quick rundown.

## Certified Dog Trainers

These are professionals trained in teaching dogs' basic obedience and addressing common behavioural issues. They usually conduct **group classes or one-on-one** training sessions.

## Certified Applied Animal Behaviorists (CAAB)

These individuals have advanced degrees in animal behaviour and are equipped to deal with more **complex behavioural issues.**

## Veterinary Behaviorists

These are vets who have undergone additional training in animal behavior. They can diagnose and treat **more serious** behavioural problems and prescribe medication if necessary.

Remember, **there's no shame in seeking help**. Sometimes, an outside perspective can provide valuable insights and new strategies.

By enlisting professional help when necessary, you're not admitting defeat; rather, you're **showing your commitment** to providing the **best possible life for your puppy**.

In this journey of learning and growth, every decision made with love and care brings us closer to a deeper bond with our faithful furry friends.

# 6. REAL-LIFE SCENARIOS AND CASE STUDIES

In this section, we'll delve into a few real-life scenarios and case studies to illustrate how behavioural issues can arise in puppies and how they can be effectively addressed.

These stories underline that **every puppy is unique, every situation is different**, and each solution is tailored to individual circumstances.

However, they all emphasize one common theme - **patience, persistence, and positivity** are key in solving behavioural problems.

## *Case Study 1: Max, The Nipping Newcomer*

Max, an energetic Border Collie, was adopted at 8 weeks old by the Johnson family. As he grew, he developed a **habit of nipping at the children**, especially during playtime. Despite several attempts to discourage this behaviour, Max continued his nipping. Eventually, the Johnsons consulted a dog trainer who advised a two-pronged approach: redirect Max's biting to suitable chew toys and use time-outs during play to reinforce that nipping meant an end to fun times.

With consistent reinforcement, Max gradually learned to play without nipping.

## *Case Study 2: Bella, The Barkstorm*

Bella, a lively Beagle puppy, was the apple of her family's eye until she developed a **relentless barking habit**. Bella would bark at all hours, at the smallest noises or sometimes for no reason at all. Concerned neighbours and sleepless nights led the family to seek help from a CAAB. The behaviourist identified Bella's **barking as a response to boredom and anxiety**.

By introducing mental stimulation toys, establishing a solid exercise routine, and applying counter-conditioning techniques to reduce anxiety, Bella's barking decreased noticeably within a few weeks.

## Case Study 3: Apollo, The Destructive Dalmatian

Apollo was a 5-month-old Dalmatian with a penchant for **destroying furniture**. His owners, after replacing three chewed-up couches, turned to a veterinary behaviourist. The behaviourist ruled out medical causes for Apollo's destructive behaviour, identifying it as a symptom of **separation anxiety**. They recommended a combination of behavior modification exercises, environmental changes, and in Apollo's case, anti-anxiety medication. The combined approach led to significant improvements, with Apollo learning to stay calm during his owners' absence.

These case studies illuminate that **each dog's behavioural issues can be unique**, and solutions are often multi-faceted.

The common denominator is always patience, persistence, and an understanding of the underlying causes.

And **remember**, it's okay to seek professional help when dealing with persistent issues.

After all, our journey with our puppies is all about ensuring their happiness and well-being. **They're not just pets; they're family.**

*Photo by **Andrea Lightfoot** on Unsplash*

# ADVANCED TRAINING

Hello there, aspiring canine experts! **If you've made it this far, give yourself a pat on the back.**

You and your puppy **have mastered** the basics of obedience, name recognition, and house training.

You've begun your journey into understanding your dog's behaviour, and how to influence it positively. Now, it's time to embark on the **fascinating path of advanced training.**

This section is your gateway to helping your furry companion reach their **full potential**.

## *Introduction to Advanced Training*

Advanced training is about more than just teaching your dog new tricks. It's a **powerful tool** that enhances communication, strengthens the bond between you and your pet, and enriches their mental stimulation. It's like a never-ending adventure for you and your dog, filled with shared achievements, understanding, and a **whole lot of fun**.

But **remember**, every dog learns **at their own pace**. So, while it's great to challenge your dog, **it's essential to maintain patience and positivity**.

## Advanced Commands and Tricks

We'll start this part by introducing **some impressive commands and tricks** such as roll over, play dead, fetch, and even agility training. Each of these exercises will come with a detailed, step-by-step guide, ensuring you can follow along and **train with ease**.

## Leash Walking and Heel

Walking on a leash is one of the most challenging skills for many dogs. We'll delve into techniques that **promote calm, focused behaviour during walks**, including the "heel" command, which instructs your dog to walk calmly by your side.

## Off-Leash Training

Imagine a scenario where your dog roams freely at the park, yet always responds to your command and returns to you. **Sounds wonderful, doesn't it?** Off-leash training can make this a reality. This chapter **will guide you** through the steps to build this trust and train your dog to **behave even when off the leash**.

## Complex Behaviors and Sequence Training

This part takes training up a notch by introducing **sequence training**, where your dog learns to perform a series of commands in a specific order. This training level will not only impress your friends but **also provide great mental stimulation for your dog**.

## The Power of Positive Reinforcement in Advanced Training

The principle of **positive reinforcement** remains the backbone of advanced training. We'll cover how to maintain this approach, keeping your training sessions as motivating and

**stress-free** as possible for your dog.

## Dealing with Training Plateaus

As with any learning process, there may be times where it feels like you and your dog aren't making progress. We'll discuss **strategies** to navigate these plateaus and keep the training process **moving forward positively**.

## Preparation for Dog Sports and Activities

For those interested in getting involved in **dog sports** such as agility, flyball, or obedience trials, we'll provide an introduction and explain how advanced training techniques can help your dog excel in these activities.

By the end of this section, you'll have a new set of tools and knowledge to expand your dog's learning and enhance your bond.

**The horizon of dog training is vast and filled with countless possibilities**, and you and your puppy are just starting the exploration.

Keep up the fantastic work, and always remember - **patience, consistency, and positive reinforcement** are your best allies on this journey. **Happy training!**

# 1. ADVANCED COMMANDS AND TRICKS

**Hey there, intrepid trainers!**

It's time to build on what we've achieved so far and **let the fun begin**.

In this section, we'll introduce you to a **variety of advanced commands and tricks** that will not only amaze your friends and family but also create an **engaging and mentally stimulating environment** for your puppy.

## Why Teach Advanced Commands and Tricks?

Beyond the show-off factor, teaching your dog advanced commands and tricks serves a **plethora of beneficial purposes**. It provides mental exercise, strengthens the bond between you two, and can even turn into a fun game for your furry friend. Plus, **remember** how we mentioned in the basics section of the first book our first book *"Puppy Training 101: A Practical Guide for Young Dog Owners"* that **dogs thrive on having a 'job' to do**?

Well, executing these tricks on command is an excellent job for them.

## Prerequisites

Before we dive into the advanced commands and tricks, **it's essential** to ensure that your dog is comfortable with **basic commands** like sit, stay, down, and come. These form the foundation upon which many advanced tricks are built.

## The "Roll Over" Trick

Let's start with a crowd-pleaser - roll over! This trick is a **progression** from the 'down' position. Through step-by-step instructions and positive reinforcement, you'll learn how to guide your puppy to roll over on your command.

## *Playing Dead*

Playing dead, or 'bang,' is another fun trick that's sure to get a reaction from anyone watching. We'll walk you through the steps and tips to train your puppy to play dead on command.

## *The "Fetch" Command*

Fetch is more than just a game. It's a great way to exercise your dog, **both mentally and physically.** We'll show you how to teach your dog to fetch an object, bring it back, and release it into your hand.

## *The "Speak" and "Quiet" Commands*

Teaching your dog when to speak (bark) and when to be quiet can be helpful, especially when dealing with excessive barking issues. We'll cover **these two commands**, teaching you how to encourage vocalization on command and silence when needed.

## *Agility Training Basics*

Agility training is a fantastic way to keep your dog **physically fit and mentally sharp**. We'll introduce you to some beginner-level agility skills, such as teaching your puppy to jump through a hoop or navigate weave poles.

**Remember**, patience and a positive attitude are key in advanced training. **It's not about how fast they learn** but about the joy and bonding during the process.

Your **puppy will likely not perfect these tricks overnight**. But with time, patience, and consistency, you'll both reap the benefits of this higher-level training.

Keep your **training sessions short and fun to keep your puppy engaged**.

Most importantly, shower them with **praise and rewards** whenever they do well. This positive reinforcement is crucial to their learning process.

So, ready to elevate your training game?

Let's dive in! You and your furry friend are going to have a blast.

# 2. THE "ROLL OVER" TRICK

Roll over, folks! It's time to dive into one of the most adorable and entertaining tricks you can teach your furry friend.

**Remember** how much fun we had training basic commands in our previous book *"Puppy Training 101: A Practical Guide for Young Dog Owners"*? Get ready for a fresh wave of joy and accomplishment as we navigate the steps to mastering the 'Roll Over' command!

## Why Teach the 'Roll Over' Command?

Apart from being a crowd-pleaser, the 'Roll Over' trick provides a great opportunity for your puppy to **stretch and exercise**. It's also a fantastic way to reinforce the **bond of trust** between you two and makes a perfect addition to your repertoire of **interactive games**.

## Prerequisites

**Before starting**, make sure your puppy has **mastered the 'down' command**. You'll be amazed at how smoothly the training goes when the 'down' command is firmly in place.

## Steps to Teach 'Roll Over'

### a. Command 'Down'

Start by commanding your puppy to 'down.' Once your pup is lying down, you're ready to move to the next step.

### b. Use a Treat

Hold a treat close to their nose, and slowly move it towards their shoulder, encouraging them to roll onto their side. As they follow the treat, **give the command 'Roll Over.'**

### c. Encourage the Roll

Continue **moving** the treat so that your puppy completes a full roll. This might take a few attempts. Keep the energy positive and your tone encouraging. **Patience is key here.**

### d. Reward

As soon as your puppy completes the roll, give them the treat and shower them with praise. It's essential to **reinforce this behaviour immediately** so they associate the trick with positive feedback.

### e. Practice

Repeat the steps above a few times each training session. Remember, **short, frequent training sessions are more effective** than long, infrequent ones.

### f. Fade Out the Lure

**Gradually** lessen the dependence on the treat, until your puppy can perform the trick without following the treat, but on hearing the command alone.

Teaching your puppy to 'Roll Over' can be a hilarious and joyful process.

**Remember**, some puppies might feel insecure exposing their belly, so make sure you're in **a quiet, comfortable space**. In time, your puppy will be rolling over like a pro, ready to wow any audience and deepen your bond even further.

Happy rolling!

# 3. THE "PLAYING DEAD" TRICK

Lights, camera, action!

Now that your puppy has mastered the "Roll Over" trick, it's time for some drama with the **highly entertaining** "Playing Dead" trick.

Let's make this **learning experience fun, engaging, and rewarding** for both you and your puppy!

## Why Teach the 'Playing Dead' Trick?

This trick is more than just a cool party piece. It's a fantastic way to encourage your dog's obedience and concentration. It also stretches and **strengthens their muscles and is a great mental exercise**.

## Prerequisites

Your dog should be comfortable with the **"Down" and "Stay" commands before starting** to learn this trick. If you need a recap, refer to the chapters dedicated to these commands in our previous book.

## Steps to Teach 'Playing Dead'

### a. Down Position

Begin by commanding your dog to lie down. They should be relaxed and comfortable in this position.

### b. Introduce the Command

Show your dog a treat and use the command "Play Dead" or "Bang!" — whichever you prefer. Hold the treat close to their nose to get their attention.

### c. Lure the Position

Move the treat from their nose towards their shoulder,

**enticing** them to roll onto their side. This is like the roll over trick, **but this time**, you want them to stay in that position.

### d. Reward the Position

Once your dog is lying on their side, give them the treat and offer lots of praise. It's crucial they associate this position and the command with a **positive outcome**.

### e. Extend the Time

**Gradually** increase the time your dog stays in the "Play Dead" position before you reward them. Use the "Stay" command to encourage them to remain still.

### f. Remove the Lure

Slowly **decrease** the use of the treat as a lure, until your dog responds to the verbal cue alone.

The "Play Dead" trick is an advanced command, and **it may take some time for your puppy to understand and respond to it consistently**.

**Remember**, patience is key! Always end training sessions on a positive note to keep your dog motivated and excited for the next session.

With **time, patience, and consistency**, your puppy will be ready for their acting debut in no time. Ready for the applause?

Let's get training!

# 4. THE "FETCH" COMMAND

Unleashing your dog's inner athlete starts with **a simple, yet powerful word**: "Fetch!"

This command is a splendid way to give your puppy a **good dose of exercise** and to strengthen your bond. **Good communication is fundamental** to successful training, and the "Fetch" command is a great example of this.

## Why Teach the 'Fetch' Command?

Apart from being an incredible way to channel your puppy's energy, the "Fetch" command promotes their **natural instinct** to retrieve, boosts their obedience skills, and provides an outlet for their mental stimulation.

## Prerequisites

Before introducing the "Fetch" command, your dog should be **comfortable with "Sit," "Stay," and "Come."** If your puppy is not familiar with these, refer to the relevant chapters in our previous book.

## Steps to Teach 'Fetch'

### a. Choose the Right Toy

Start with a toy that your dog loves. It can be a ball, a stuffed animal, or any **safe object** they enjoy playing with.

### b. Engage Your Dog

Get your dog's attention by playing with the toy. Make it seem **interesting and fun**.

### c. Throw the Toy

With your dog's attention on the toy, throw it a **short distance** away while clearly saying the command "Fetch!"

### d. Encourage the Retrieve

At first, your puppy might run to the toy and not bring it back.

**Don't worry**! Encourage them to return with the toy using their name and an **enthusiastic tone**.

### e.  Command 'Drop it'

Once your dog returns to you with the toy, use the command "Drop it." If necessary, you can exchange the toy for a treat to reinforce this behaviour.

### f.  Repeat and Reward

**Keep repeating** this sequence. When your dog successfully fetches and returns the toy and reward them with a treat and lots of praise.

**Remember**, just like teaching any new command, **the process takes patience, repetition, and lots of positive reinforcement**. Always make sure your training sessions are fun and engaging.

Soon, your fetch games will be the highlight of your puppy's day and a fun activity to share with family and friends.

Let's get ready to fetch!

# 5. THE "SPEAK" AND "QUIET" COMMANDS

Welcome to the symphony of puppyhood, where our little furry friends 'speak' in barks and whines!

Learning how to control this choir with the "Speak" and "Quiet" commands is a big step towards creating a **harmonious relationship** with your puppy.

## Why Teach the 'Speak' and 'Quiet' Commands?

These commands are critical in managing your puppy's vocalization. It's not about suppressing their natural instinct to bark, but rather, **it's about teaching them to bark on command and cease when instructed**. This is particularly helpful in circumstances where their barking could be disruptive or unwelcome.

## Prerequisites

Before introducing these commands, **your dog should be comfortable with "Sit," "Stay," and "Come."** If not, I recommend refreshing these skills by revisiting our previous guide.

## Steps to Teach 'Speak' and 'Quiet'

### a. Stimulate a Bark

Find a situation that **naturally makes your puppy bark**. It could be the doorbell ringing or the sight of a toy.

### b. Introduce the 'Speak' Command

Once your puppy starts barking, calmly say "Speak" and reward them with a treat. Be sure to only give the treat when they bark, reinforcing the **connection** between the command and the action.

### c. Introduce the 'Quiet' Command

After your puppy understands the "Speak" command, it's time to teach them to be quiet. Once they start barking on command, say "Quiet" in a calm and assertive voice. You **might need** to wait a bit until they naturally stop barking.

### d. Reward the Silence

The moment they stop barking, **immediately** give them a treat and praise them. This helps them associate the command "Quiet" with stopping their barking.

### e. Repeat and Practice

Keep repeating these steps until your puppy can "Speak" and be "Quiet" on command. Remember, **practice is crucial, and patience is your best ally**.

**Remember** that these commands are not intended to prevent your puppy from ever barking. Dogs bark to communicate. Instead, use these **commands to help manage excessive or inappropriate barking.**

**Don't forget**, you're not just training a puppy; **you're nurturing a bond based on mutual trust and respect**. Every bark and every silence is a note in the song of your life together.

Keep practicing, keep playing, and keep enjoying every moment of this beautiful journey.

Happy training!

# 6. AGILITY TRAINING BASICS

Hello, future agility stars!

Well, now we're about to take things up a notch and introduce the exciting world of agility training.

This isn't just about showing off your puppy's skills at the dog park – **it's about teamwork, bonding, and keeping your furry friend physically and mentally stimulated**.

## What is Agility Training?

Agility training is a dog sport that involves a handler directing a dog **through various obstacles** such as tunnels, teeter-totters, and jumps. It's not just for those who wish to compete; it's a fun and rewarding way to exercise and bond with your dog.

## Benefits of Agility Training

### a. Physical Exercise

Agility training is a high-energy activity that helps keep your puppy **fit, agile, and healthy**.

### b. Mental Stimulation

The variety of tasks in agility training ensures your **puppy's mind stays sharp and engaged**.

### c. Confidence Building

Overcoming obstacles and learning new tasks can significantly boost your puppy's **confidence**.

### d. Deepens Your Bond

Working together in agility training strengthens the **connection** between you and your puppy.

## Starting Agility Training

**Remember**, safety comes first. Puppies' joints and bones are still developing, and jumping too high or running too hard can cause damage. **For young puppies, start with ground-level exercises and low-impact obstacles**. Consider consulting with a vet before beginning any rigorous training regimen.

## *Here's how to get started*

### a. Warm-Up

Start every training session with a short warm-up to get your puppy ready for action.

### b. Start with Simple Obstacles

Begin with easy tasks such as going through a tunnel or weaving between cones. **Make sure** your puppy masters these before moving on to more challenging obstacles.

### c. Use Positive Reinforcement

Always reward your puppy with treats, praise, or playtime whenever they successfully navigate an obstacle.

### d. Keep Training Sessions Short

Young **puppies have short attention spans**. Keep training sessions to around 10-15 minutes at first.

### e. Patience and Consistency

It takes time to build agility skills. Stay **patient, consistent**, and always end training sessions on a **positive note**.

Exploring agility training opens a whole new world of activities for you and your puppy. It's a journey that leads to a more confident, agile, and happy dog, and a deeper, more **rewarding bond for both of you**.

So, let's get out there, have some fun, and show the world what you and your buddy can do!

# 7. LEASH WALKING AND 'HEEL' COMMAND

**Hello again, dog enthusiasts!**

As you continue this wonderful journey of training your puppy, we've come to a topic that's **fundamental for your daily walks and outdoor adventures** - leash walking and the 'Heel' command.

We are now ready to elevate those skills!

## Why is Leash Walking and the 'Heel' Command Important?

Walking on a leash comfortably and **the command 'Heel' are crucial for the safety and manners of your puppy**. When mastered, it ensures that your dog walks politely by your side without pulling, straining, or leading the way.

This training is not only beneficial for walks but is also essential in crowded places, crossing streets, or **whenever you need to keep your puppy close and controlled**.

## Steps for Training Your Puppy to Walk on a Leash and 'Heel'

### a. Introduce the Leash and Collar

Let your puppy get used to wearing a collar and leash. Start by letting them wear it during play and feeding times, associating it with **positive experiences**.

### b. Start Indoors

Begin leash training indoors where there are fewer distractions. Let your puppy lead the way and explore while gently guiding them. **Reward** their cooperation with treats and praise.

### c. Teach the 'Heel' Command

With your puppy on the leash, hold a treat in your hand close to your side and say 'Heel'. Walk a few steps. If your puppy stays by your side, give them the treat and praise. Over time, **increase the distance** you walk before rewarding.

### d. Practice Makes Perfect

Take the **training outside**, starting in a quiet place with few distractions. Gradually build up to busier environments, all the while reinforcing the 'Heel' command.

### e. Patience is Key

**Remember**, this is advanced training. **Progress may be slow**, but with patience, consistency, and positive reinforcement, your puppy will catch on.

Walking with your puppy at 'Heel' is an enjoyable experience that enhances the bond between you. It allows for safer, more controlled walks, and is a great way to exhibit your **puppy's good manners.**

Keep sessions short, fun, and positive. Most importantly, enjoy the journey and celebrate every step forward – however small it might seem.

**Keep going; you're doing a fantastic job!**

*Photo by **Alvan Nee** on **Unsplash***

# 8. OFF-LEASH TRAINING

**Greetings, aspiring dog trainers!**

We've made a fantastic journey together through leash training and introducing the 'Heel' command. Now, it's time to take another giant leap and dive into the world of off-leash training.

**Yes, it's as exciting as it sounds!** But **remember, gradual progress, consistency, and a dash of patience** are the secret ingredients to successful training.

## *The Importance of Off-Leash Training*

**Imagine** hiking with your dog through beautiful trails, or enjoying a day at the beach, without the constant tension of a leash. That's the freedom off-leash training can bring.

**This level of training opens a world of possibilities for outdoor adventures** with your dog. It also indicates an **impressive level of trust** between you and your furry friend and signifies your dog's obedience and understanding of commands even without physical restraint.

## *Step-by-Step Guide to Off-Leash Training*

### a. Master Basic Commands

Your dog should be proficient in basic commands like 'Sit,' 'Stay,' 'Come,' and 'Leave It.' These commands are crucial for off-leash control.

### b. Start with a Long Leash

Before going completely off-leash, **use a long leash or a retractable one**. This gives your dog a taste of freedom while you still have control.

### c. Gradually Increase Distances

Practice commands with increasing distances between you and your dog. Praise and reward them for obeying commands from afar.

### d. Try Off-Leash in a Controlled Environment

Begin off-leash training in a safe, enclosed space like a backyard or an off-leash dog park.

### e. Practice Recall Religiously

'Come' is arguably the most crucial command for off-leash training. **Practice it extensively,** rewarding your dog every time they return to you.

### f. Be Patient and Consistent

Progress can be slow, and there may be setbacks. **Stay patient and consistent**, and celebrate small victories along the way.

Off-leash training is **an advanced skill, both for you and your dog**.

**Don't rush the process**.

Take one step at a time, making sure your dog is comfortable and confident at each stage before moving forward. **Your safety and your dog's safety** should always be your top priority.

**Remember**, this journey is as much about the destination as it is about the bond you're building with your canine companion. **You're not just training a dog**; you're creating memories and establishing a friendship that will last a lifetime.

Keep going, and remember to enjoy the journey.
**You're doing an amazing job!**

# 9. COMPLEX BEHAVIORS AND SEQUENCE TRAINING

Hello, enthusiastic trainers! You've come a long way in your training journey, mastering basic and advanced commands, and even off-leash training.

It's time now **to embark on another exciting adventure** – training complex behaviours and sequences.

This is where you can truly appreciate **the intelligence and capability of your canine companion**.

Before we begin, let me **reassure you** that while this may sound daunting, **it's nothing you can't handle.**

**Remember**, training is a journey that you and your dog embark on together. It's about **communication, patience, and enjoying each step along the way.**

## What are Complex Behaviors?

Complex behaviours are actions that require your dog **to perform several steps in order, usually in response to a single command**. They may include routines like fetching a particular item, closing a door, or even performing a trick sequence.

## Training Complex Behaviors

Training complex behaviours involves a **technique known as "chaining,"** which breaks down a behaviour into individual steps, each of which becomes a separate command.

**Here's how you can do it:**

**a. Identify the Behavior**

First, decide on the complex behaviour you want to train. Make sure it's something within your **dog's physical abilities** and is safe.

**b. Break It Down**

Break the behaviour down into **manageable parts**. For example, if you're training your dog to fetch your slippers, the sequence might be: 'Find Slippers,' 'Pick Up,' 'Come,' 'Drop.'

### c. Train Each Part Separately

Use **positive reinforcement** to train each step of the sequence as a separate command, just like you would any other command.

### d. Link the Commands

Start to **gradually** link the commands together. **Practice two steps at a time**, rewarding your dog only when both are completed correctly.

### e. Practice the Full Chain

Once your dog is comfortable with the separate steps, **practice the full chain** of behaviours. Make sure to keep the training sessions short and fun!

### f. Add a Cue

Finally, add a specific command or hand signal that will prompt the entire sequence.

## Patience and Consistency are Key

**Remember**, this level of training is quite advanced and can be challenging for both you and your dog.

It's essential **to be patient, consistent, and keep the training sessions positive and enjoyable**. Celebrate every tiny victory and don't forget to **take breaks and have fun**.

Keep in mind, we're not just training our dogs to perform complex behaviours for our convenience or amusement. We're also providing them with mental stimulation, strengthening our bond with them, and helping them **understand that they are a valued and integral part of our lives.**

**Remember**, you're doing an incredible job.

**Keep going, stay patient,** and enjoy this wonderful journey

**with your furry friend!**

# 10. THE POWER OF POSITIVE REINFORCEMENT IN ADVANCED TRAINING

**Hello, dedicated trainers!**

If you've journeyed with us this far, you've already seen the power of positive reinforcement in action.

As we delve into advanced training, **let's explore how this method becomes even more vital and effective.**

In our previous book, "*Puppy Training 101: A Practical Guide for Young Dog Owners*", we discussed the importance of **positive reinforcement in establishing the basics of training**. In essence, it is a method where we reward the behaviours we want to see more of, encouraging our dogs to repeat them.

**Positive reinforcement** can include treats, praises, pets, or anything else your dog loves. The reinforcement is the 'positive' element introduced to increase the likelihood of the desired behaviour.

## *Positive Reinforcement in Advanced Training*

As we progress into advanced training, the behaviours we seek to train become **more complex, challenging, and require a higher level of focus from our dogs.** This is where positive reinforcement truly shines.

### a. Building on Existing Behaviors

Advanced training often involves extending or combining behaviours your dog already knows.

For example, 'stay' becomes 'stay until I return,' and 'fetch' becomes 'fetch the newspaper.' When your dog performs these advanced actions, a well-timed reward reinforces the behaviour and encourages them to repeat it.

### b. Encouraging Willing Participation

Complex behaviours can be mentally challenging. Positive reinforcement keeps training sessions exciting and rewarding for your dog, motivating them to engage and **participate willingly**.

### c. Improving Focus and Concentration

Rewarding your dog for correct behaviours helps them **maintain focus and enhances their concentration** during training sessions.

This is **crucial** for mastering advanced behaviours and commands.

### d. Creating a Strong Bond

When your dog associates training with rewards and positive experiences, it fosters a deeper bond between you. This bond is essential for advanced training where your dog needs to **trust your guidance** implicitly.

### e. Increasing Confidence

**Successfully** learning advanced commands and tricks can boost your dog's confidence, making them more eager to learn new things.

## Using Positive Reinforcement Effectively

The effectiveness of positive reinforcement hinges on **timing and consistency**. The reward must immediately follow the desired behaviour so your dog can make the connection. Being consistent ensures your dog understands what behaviour is being rewarded.

**Remember**, all dogs are different. What works as a positive reinforcer for one might not work for another. Some dogs might work for treats, while others prefer a game of fetch or a good belly rub.

Lastly, as we advance in training, our ultimate aim is to **gradually reduce the reliance on treats** and move towards other forms of rewards such as **praise, petting, or playtime**. This encourages your dog to perform behaviours for the joy of interaction and approval, rather than just for treats.

As you navigate this advanced training journey, **always remember the power of positivity.** The positive reinforcement approach is more than just a training tool; it's a way of communicating love, approval, and mutual respect with your furry friend.

**Keep training sessions fun, exciting, and reward-filled**. After all, a motivated and happy dog is a joy to train!

# 11. DEALING WITH TRAINING PLATEAUS

Dear dedicated trainers, **congratulations on making it this far!**

Through this journey, we've seen your puppy transform from an adorable little bundle of energy into a well-trained companion. **However**, you may have encountered or will soon meet a phase in training that can **feel frustrating**: the training plateau.

**Not to worry,** though. It's **a completely normal part of the training process**.

This section is dedicated to helping you **understand and overcome** training plateaus effectively.

A training plateau is a stage where it seems like your dog isn't making any further progress despite your consistent efforts. **It can occur at any stage**, but it's particularly common in advanced training due to the complexity of the behaviours we're teaching.

## Why Training Plateaus Occur

Several factors contribute to training plateaus:

### a. Overwhelming Complexity

If the command is **too complex**, your dog might struggle to understand what you're asking. It's like learning a complicated dance routine; you need to master the steps before you can perform the whole sequence.

### b. Inconsistency

Consistency is key in dog training. If there are inconsistencies in your training method, your dog may become **confused** about what behaviour is expected.

### c. Fatigue or Boredom

Like us, dogs can also experience **mental fatigue or boredom**. If the training sessions are too long or the same routine is repeated too many times, your dog might lose interest.

## Overcoming the Plateau

**Don't let a plateau discourage you**; it's merely a signal to change your approach.

Here are some strategies:

### a. Break It Down

If the command is complex, break it down into smaller, manageable parts. Reward your dog for mastering each part before moving on to the next. This process is known as **'shaping'**.

### b. Consistency is Crucial

Ensure you're consistent with your commands, hand signals, and rewards. Changes in these can **confuse your dog**.

### c. Keep Training Sessions Short and Fun

To prevent boredom or fatigue, keep training sessions short, about 5 to 15 minutes. Multiple short sessions in a day are better than one long session. **Remember** to keep it fun, too. If your dog enjoys the training, they're more likely to engage and learn.

### d. Change the Environment

Sometimes, a change of scenery can do wonders. If your dog has been practicing in the same place, try moving to a **new location**. This not only keeps training exciting but also helps your dog generalize the commands in different settings.

### e. Take a Break

It's okay to take a break if things are getting **too stressful**. A day off can give you and your dog a much-needed reset.

### f. Celebrate Small Wins

**Be patient**, and celebrate even the smallest progress. This encourages your dog and keeps the training atmosphere positive.

**Remember**, every dog is unique. They learn at **their own pace** and have their own strengths and challenges.

Embrace the journey, be patient, and always **remember** to celebrate the progress you've made. After all, the ultimate goal is not perfection but to **strengthen your bond** and enjoy this amazing journey together.

**Keep going, you're doing great!**

# 12. PREPARATION FOR DOG SPORTS AND ACTIVITIES

It's a thrilling moment in your journey, dear trainers!

Now that your furry friend has mastered basic and advanced commands, it's time to **raise the stakes** and venture into the exciting realm of dog sports and activities.

This section will provide you with **a comprehensive guide** on how to prepare your dog for a variety of dog sports and activities, highlighting the benefits, the preparation process, and tips for success.

## *Why Dog Sports and Activities?*

Dog sports and activities provide an excellent platform for your dog to utilize their skills, burn off energy, and stimulate their minds. It also strengthens the bond between you and your dog as you work as a team.

Whether it's agility, obedience trials, flyball, or herding, these activities can cater to the specific instincts and interests of different breeds and individual dogs.

**They're a fun way** to take your dog's training to the next level!

## *Preparation*

### a. Choose the Right Activity

First, you need to pick the right activity. **Consider** your dog's breed, size, personality, and preferences. Some dogs might excel in activities that require speed and agility, while others might be more suited to tasks that require patience and precision.

### b. Health Check

Always consult with your veterinarian before you start any rigorous training program. It's essential to ensure your dog is healthy and fit for the activity you've chosen.

### c. Basic and Advanced Obedience

A strong foundation of basic and advanced obedience training is essential. Your dog should be **able to follow commands** reliably in different environments.

### d. Conditioning

Like any athlete, your dog will need to be **physically** conditioned for the chosen sport or activity. This could involve regular exercise, strength training, and specific exercises to improve agility or precision.

### e. Equipment

Depending on the activity, you may need to invest in specific equipment, such as jumps, tunnels, or scent articles.

### f. Socialization

If the chosen activity involves interaction with other dogs or people, ensure your dog is **well-socialized and comfortable** in these situations.

## *Training*

Training for dog sports and activities can be a fun and rewarding process. **Remember** to keep training sessions positive and enjoyable for your dog. Always use rewards-based methods and avoid harsh corrections.

**Patience is key—don't rush the process**.

Practice regularly, but also make sure to give your dog **plenty of time to rest and recover**. Overtraining can lead to stress and injuries. Always end on **a positive note** to keep your dog enthusiastic about training.

Joining a **local club or hiring a trainer** with experience in the chosen activity can be hugely beneficial. They can guide you through the training process, provide helpful tips, and offer support.

**Remember**, the main goal of these activities is to have fun and strengthen the bond between you and your dog.

Winning competitions or earning titles is a bonus, but the **real reward** lies in the journey you share with your canine buddy.

So embrace this new adventure, and let's create some amazing memories together!

*Photo by **Ayla Verschueren** on Unsplash*

# HEALTHCARE

As we embark on the exciting journey of advanced training and fun activities with our canine companions, it is crucial that we never lose sight of one of the most vital components of their wellbeing – **healthcare**.

**Welcome, dear readers**, to the healthcare section of our guide.

Here, we'll delve into the necessary steps you should take to ensure your **puppy grows into a healthy and happy adult dog.** As always, our aim is to give you the knowledge to care for your dog's health confidently and proactively, paving the way for many joy-filled years ahead.

**Never forget** that a dog's happiness is rooted in its health, and a happy dog makes for an ecstatic dog parent!

## Routine Vet Check-ups

**Regular** vet visits are not just for when your dog is unwell. They form a significant part of **preventative** healthcare. A professional vet can **spot early signs** of potential health issues before they become severe problems, much like regular check-ups with your doctor help maintain your health.

## *Vaccinations*

Vaccinations are crucial in protecting your pup from various diseases. Consult with your vet about the necessary vaccines and the right schedule for them. **Common vaccinations** include rabies, distemper, parvovirus, and adenovirus.

## *Parasite Control*

Ticks, heartworms, fleas and other parasites can cause serious health problems for your dog. **Fortunately**, with regular preventative measures, these issues can be avoided. There are many effective products on the market to control and prevent infestations.

## *Dental Care*

Oral hygiene isn't only important for us humans; it's also vital for our pets. **Dental diseases** in dogs can lead to severe health complications. **Regularly** brush your dog's teeth, provide dental chews, and have check-ups with the vet.

## *Balanced Diet and Exercise*

A balanced diet is the basis of good health for your pup. Ensure your dog's food meets all their **nutritional requirements** and is appropriate for their age, size, and breed. Combine this with regular exercise to keep your dog physically fit and mentally stimulated.

## *Grooming*

Grooming isn't just about keeping your puppy looking their best; it's also an essential aspect of their overall health. **Regular grooming**, including brushing the fur, trimming the nails, and checking ears, can help **prevent potential health issues**.

## *Mental Health*

Mental health is very vital, just as important as physical health. Make sure your dog has plenty of **stimulation** and isn't left alone for extended periods. Training, socialization, playtime, and cuddles are all excellent for your dog's mental well-being.

## *Senior Dogs*

As dogs age, their health needs will change. Senior dogs may require different diets, more frequent vet check-ups, and alterations to their exercise routines. They may also require more rest and **specific** accommodations for any health conditions they have.

**Remember**, always consult with your vet about your dog's healthcare. They can provide specific advice tailored to your dog's needs and circumstances. Your vet is your ally in your quest to provide the best possible care for your pup, so build a strong, open line of **communication** with them.

Let's emphasize the power of **love and consistency in training** your new pup. The same applies to healthcare.

**With regular check-ups, preventative care**, and a lot of love, you can ensure that your furry friend enjoys a long, healthy, and fulfilling life by your side.

So let's embark on this vital part of the journey together, ensuring our dogs have the vibrant and active life they deserve!

# 1. ROUTINE VET CHECK-UPS

Welcome to the first section of our **Healthcare** chapter, where we'll be talking about the cornerstone of your dog's healthcare regimen - Routine Vet Check-ups.

Just as we, humans, need to make **regular trips to the doctor**, our furry friends need the same care and attention to stay at their healthiest and happiest.

As dog owners, we must take our role seriously, not only as their best friend but as **their primary caregiver as well**.

You'll be the first to notice any **changes in behaviour or appearance** that may suggest a potential health concern. However, it's important to remember that not all health problems are immediately visible to the untrained eye, and this is where **regular vet visits come in**.

Vet visits should not be considered solely as reactive measures to sickness. Rather, they play a vital role in the **preventive healthcare** of your pup. Much like our routine health checks, these visits can help in the early detection of potential health issues before they escalate.

**Remember**, prevention is always better than cure!

During a routine check-up, your vet will do a thorough physical examination, **checking everything** from your dog's eyes, ears, and mouth to their heart, lungs, and abdomen. They'll also check your dog's weight, skin and coat health, and may also take routine blood tests. This **comprehensive examination** can spot signs of potential problems that are **not visible** from the surface.

Regular vet check-ups are especially **crucial during the puppy stages** when your dog will be getting vaccinated. As your dog matures, these visits may focus more on preventive care and early detection of the diseases that can affect adult and older dogs.

It's very important to build an open and trusting relationship with your vet. **Don't hesitate to ask questions or voice any concerns** you may have.

**Remember**, no one knows your dog better than you do, and your observations can help the vet provide the best care possible.

The **frequency** of the vet visits will depend on your dog's age, breed, and health condition. Puppies and senior dogs usually require more frequent check-ups, while healthy adult dogs may only need an annual visit.

However, **your vet will guide you** on the most appropriate schedule for your pup.

With routine vet check-ups, you can feel confident in the knowledge that you're doing your utmost to safeguard your dog's health.

It might seem like a small thing, but these regular visits can make a **massive difference** in your dog's quality of life, potentially spotting issues early and keeping them happier and by **your side for longer**.

**Consistency is key**, and it applies equally to healthcare as it does to training. Your consistent effort in taking care of your dog's health will result in **a healthy, happy** dog who's ready to embark on all sorts of adventures with you.

Let's take this important step in our journey, showing our pups how much we love and care for them, **one vet visit at a time!**

# 2. VACCINATIONS

Continuing our journey through the fundamental aspects of your dog's healthcare, let's delve into an important topic that can sometimes cause a **lot of questions and concerns** for new pet parents - Vaccinations.

## *Let's start with the basics*

**What exactly are vaccinations?**

In a nutshell, vaccines **help prepare** your pup's immune system to defend against harmful diseases. They contain antigens, which mimic disease-causing organisms in your dog's body but don't actually cause illness. Instead, they prompt the immune system to **develop protection** against the specific diseases the vaccines are designed for.

Vaccinations are a **crucial part of your dog's health** regimen. They protect your pup from severe, sometimes deadly diseases like rabies, parvovirus, distemper, and leptospirosis, among others.

Just like in humans, these preventative measures are worth their weight in gold, keeping your pup healthy, happy, and safe from common canine ailments.

Puppy vaccinations start **as early as six to eight weeks old and continue until they're about 16 weeks old**. After this initial series of vaccinations, your dog will typically require annual or triennial booster shots, depending on the vaccine and your vet's recommendations.

The idea of vaccinating a little puppy **might seem daunting**, but rest assured, these are routine procedures performed by your trusted vet. **Remember** that your vet is there to ensure the well-being of your pup and is always available to address **any concerns or questions** you may have about the process.

We understand that the world of vaccines **can seem**

**complicated** with terms like 'core vaccines', 'non-core vaccines', 'puppy shots', and 'booster shots'. Don't let these confuse you.

## Here's a brief explanation

- **Core vaccines** are those recommended for every dog, regardless of their lifestyle, location, or breed. These typically include vaccines for rabies, distemper, parvovirus, and adenovirus.

- **Non-core** vaccines are given based on your dog's risk factors. These may include vaccines for diseases like Bordetella (also known as kennel cough), Lyme disease, or leptospirosis.

- **Puppy shots** refer to the series of vaccines given to your pup during their first few months.

- **Booster shots** are the subsequent doses that your dog will receive after their initial vaccination schedule to ensure they remain protected throughout their life.

In the spirit of the **positive, can-do attitude** approach vaccinations with the same optimistic outlook. It's a vital part of being a responsible pet parent, and it paves the way for many healthy, adventurous years to come with your four-legged friend.

**Remember**, you're not alone in this journey.

Your vet is your partner and will guide you through the vaccination process, explaining which vaccines are essential for your dog, when they should be administered, and how often they should be renewed.

Every step we take in this journey of pet parenthood, no matter how small it might seem, contributes to a **healthier and happier life** for our canine companions.

So let's make sure we're providing our pups with **the best care**

**we can give** - because they would do the same for us!

# 3. PARASITE CONTROL

As we continue our journey through the world of canine healthcare, let's talk about a topic that might make your skin crawl a little – **Parasite Control.**

**Don't fret, though**! Just like with training, understanding, and knowing how to prevent and treat these pesky intruders can make all the difference for your furry friend's wellbeing.

Dogs, as **adventurous and curious creatures** as they are, can sometimes bring unwanted guests back home. These can include **external parasites** like fleas and ticks, or **internal parasites** like heartworms, roundworms, and tapeworms. **The good news?** With the right knowledge and care, we can **keep these potential nuisances at bay!**

So, let's dive into the world of parasite control with the same **positive and motivated mindset** we've been fostering since we began this journey.

**Fleas and ticks** are the mainstream external parasites in dogs. Besides causing itchiness and discomfort, they **can also transmit diseases**. Fleas can cause flea allergy dermatitis, and a heavy infestation can lead to anemia in puppies. Ticks can spread conditions like Lyme disease or tick fever.

**To protect your dog** from these pests, regular use of preventive products is key. These can be in the form of spot-on treatments, oral medications, or collars infused with a preventive. **Establishing routines** is not only beneficial for training, it's also a **lifesaver** in healthcare, including parasite control!

When it comes to internal parasites, prevention is also the best medicine. **Heartworms** are transmitted through mosquito bites, and they can cause severe heart and lung disease. **Roundworms** and **tapeworms** can lead to digestive issues and malnutrition. Regular testing and preventive medication can protect your dog from these internal threats.

Your vet will play a critical role in guiding you through parasite control.

They can identify to you the best products based on your dog's age, weight, health status, and lifestyle. **Remember**, your vet is a part of your dog's health team - they're there to support and guide you every step of the way!

Regular grooming and health checks are also part of good parasite control. For example, **brushing your dog's coat** frequently and checking for ticks after an outdoor adventure can help catch potential problems early.

It's important to **remember** that taking steps for parasite control is not a sign of a dirty or poorly cared for dog – **even the most pampered pooches** can pick up pests. Instead, it's an essential part of comprehensive healthcare and responsible pet parenting.

Our dogs give us their absolute best every day – their love, their trust, their never-ending tail wags. In return, it's up to us to provide them with the best care, and that includes protecting them from tiny invaders.

Together, we can ensure our furry friends live **their happiest, healthiest lives!**

# 4. DENTAL CARE

A sweet puppy's breath and their adorable little teeth – there's nothing quite like it!

**Just like us**, our canine friends need good dental care to ensure those cute chompers stay healthy and strong.

Maintaining good oral health is a **serious part** of your dog's overall well-being and can even add years to their lives. It may seem daunting, **but don't worry!**

We're here to guide you through the process, and together we'll ensure your furry friend has a clean and gleaming smile.

**Firstly**, let's understand why dental care is so crucial.

Dental disease is more than simply bad breath – it's **the most common disease in dogs**, affecting 80% of all canines by the age of two. Left untreated, dental disease could lead to pain, tooth loss, and even serious systemic issues like heart disease and kidney problems.

**But there's great news!**

Dental disease is entirely preventable with **good dental care habits**.

Brushing your dog's teeth might seem odd, but it's the gold standard in pet dental care. It's never too late to start, **but the earlier, the better**.

Turning brushing into a fun and **positive experience** can help make this an enjoyable routine for both you and your pup.

To brush your dog's teeth, use a **dog-specific toothbrush and toothpaste**. At no time use human toothpaste, as it contains ingredients that could be harmful to your dog.

Start slow and **gradually increase** the brushing time as your dog becomes more comfortable. Aim to brush your dog's teeth daily, but even a few times a week can make a big difference.

**Dental chews** and a balanced diet can also play a part in your dog's dental health. Dental chews can help reduce tartar and plaque, while a balanced diet promotes overall health, including dental health. **However**, they are **not a substitute** for brushing and professional cleanings.

Regular professional dental cleanings at your vet are also crucial. Your vet will clean and polish your dog's teeth, and they'll be able to spot and address potential issues before they become big problems. **Consider** these cleanings as your pup's personal 'spa days' – an essential part of their care routine!

As with all aspects of our journey, **patience and persistence** are key.

**Don't get discouraged** if your dog doesn't take to toothbrushing immediately. Keep **sessions short, stay positive**, and reward your dog for their cooperation. In time, they will come to see toothbrushing as just another enjoyable part of their day.

Taking care of your dog's teeth may not be the first thing you think of when you consider pet care, but **its impact is wide-reaching**

A healthy mouth means a happier, healthier dog. And that's what we're all here for – to give our furry friends the best life possible.

Let's get brushing and give our pups a reason to 'smile'!

# 5. BALANCED DIET AND EXERCISE

There's an old saying that goes, **"You are what you eat."** The same can be said for our four-legged friends, and their lifestyle plays an equally important role.

**A balanced diet combined with regular exercise** are two the most crucial elements for your dog's overall health and well-being. This dynamic duo is the backbone of a vibrant and healthy life for your pup.

It's about more than just keeping your dog fit and trim—it impacts their mood, energy levels, **longevity**, and even the shine on their coat!

As the proud caregiver of a young dog, you have the golden opportunity to instill these **healthy habits** from the start.

Let's dive in and discover how you can champion this cause.

## Balanced Diet

Choosing the right food for your dog might feel like navigating a labyrinth. There are countless options, each claiming to be the best. **Don't worry—you're not alone** in this journey, and we're here to shed some light.

First, choose a dog food that is **"complete and balanced"**.

This means it should include, encompass all the nutrients your dog needs in the correct ratios. This is typically indicated on the label. **Remember, puppies and adult dogs have different nutritional needs**, so make sure the food is appropriate for your dog's life stage.

Your **dog's breed, size, age, and health status** will influence the type of diet they should be on. It's always best to **consult with your vet** about this, as they can provide personalized advice based on your dog's unique needs.

**Fresh water should be always available**. Dehydration might quickly lead to serious health problems.

**Treats** are also part of your dog's diet. While it's okay to indulge your dog with a treat occasionally, remember that these should make up **no more than 10%** of your dog's total caloric intake.

## *Exercise*

Now, let's move on to the 'E' word—exercise.

Regular physical activity is **essential** for your pup. It aids in maintaining a healthy weight, keeps their heart healthy, and even helps curb behavioural problems by keeping them **mentally stimulated**.

Puppies are bundles of energy, but their bodies are still growing. **Short**, frequent play sessions are best. As your dog matures, you can gradually increase the duration and intensity of the exercise.

**Each dog is an individual**, and the amount and type of exercise they need can vary based on their age, breed, and health.

**Generally**, dogs should get at least 1 hour of exercise each day, but some active breeds may require more.

Exercise isn't just about physical health; it also provides an excellent opportunity for **training and socialization.**

Teaching your dog to fetch or play hide-and-seek can stimulate their mind and strengthen your bond. Group activities like **hiking or visiting dog parks** can help your dog discover how to **interact appropriately** with humans and other dogs.

**Bringing it all together**, a balanced diet and regular exercise can work wonders on your dog's health, behaviour, and quality of life

**Consistency is key**. Establishing a regular feeding and exercise schedule can create a positive routine for your dog.

Remember, **you're your dog's role model**. If you approach diet and exercise with positivity and enthusiasm, your dog is likely to follow suit. Your furry friend trusts you to make the best decisions for them—they're relying on you to lead the way to a healthy, happy life.

**Let's make them proud!**

# 6. GROOMING

Grooming is more than just keeping your dog looking their best—it's an **essential part** of their overall health and wellness.

**Proper** grooming helps keep your dog clean, reduces the risk of skin conditions, and gives you an opportunity to look for any abnormalities such as lumps, ticks, or issues with their eyes, ears, or teeth.

So, **grab your brush**, because we're about to dive into the fantastic world of dog grooming!

## Coat Care

**Regular brushing** is crucial for all dogs, regardless of the length of their coat. Not only does brushing remove dead hair and mats, but it also spreads natural oils throughout the coat, keeping it healthy and shiny.

**The frequency of brushing** will depend on your dog's breed and coat type—some dogs may require daily brushing, while others may only need a good brush-out once a week.

When it comes to **bathing**, the rule is: **not too often, not too rare**. Over-bathing can remove the natural oils from your dog's skin, leading to dryness and irritation. On the other hand, under-bathing can lead to a build-up of dirt and oils, causing skin problems.

Most dogs need **a bath about once a month**, but your vet can guide you based on your dog's specific needs.

## Nail Trimming

**Dog nails need regular trimming** to prevent them from getting too long. Overgrown nails can lead to problems with their posture and walking, and can **also be painful for your dog**. The frequency of nail trims will depend on your dog's lifestyle and how quickly their nails grow.

Typically, most dogs will need a **nail trim once a month**.

Nail trimming can be a **nerve-wracking experience for both dogs and humans**, especially because dog nails have a 'quick' that can bleed if cut. It's essential to approach this task with calmness and confidence.

If you're unsure about how to do it, seek advice from your vet or **a professional groomer**. With patience and practice, nail trimming can **become a stress-free routine**.

## *Ear and Eye Care*

**Ears and eyes are sensitive areas** that need gentle care.

Check your **dog's ears weekly** for any signs of redness, swelling, or a bad smell that could indicate an infection. Some dogs, especially those with **floppy ears**, may need regular ear cleanings.

Your dog's eyes should be **clear and bright**. If you notice redness, cloudiness, or excessive tear production, it's **time to consult the vet**.

**Remember, positive reinforcement**, It applies to grooming, too!

Make sure to associate **grooming practices with positive experiences** for your dog. **Treats, praises, or playtime** can make grooming something your dog looks forward to, **not something they dread**.

Your commitment to regular grooming not only ensures that your dog looks great but also keeps them **healthy and happy**. Plus, it's a fantastic opportunity to bond with your furry friend.

Now go ahead, grab that brush, **and let the grooming fun begin!**

# 7. MENTAL HEALTH

In the grand adventure of dog ownership, it's easy to focus heavily on physical health and training while overlooking another critical aspect: **mental health.**

Dogs, like humans, **have emotional needs that must be addressed** to ensure they're not just surviving but truly thriving.

Let's delve into the **fascinating world** of canine mental health and explore how we can enrich our dogs' minds.

## Mental Stimulation

Dogs are **intelligent creatures** that require mental stimulation to keep their minds sharp and avoid boredom. **Mental stimulation** can be provided in many ways, such as interactive toys, puzzle feeders, learning new commands, or agility training.

**Remember** the "Fetch" command we discussed in the Advanced Training section? It's not just about physical exercise. **It's also about working their minds** as they learn to understand and follow your commands.

You can also stimulate your dog's mind by **changing up your walking routine. Exploring a new route or park** introduces your dog to a variety of new smells and sights, keeping their brain engaged and alert.

## Reducing Stress and Anxiety

Dogs can experience stress and anxiety, **much like humans.**

This can result from **various factors**, such as changes in the environment, separation anxiety, or fear of loud noises like thunderstorms or fireworks. Learning to recognize signs of stress in your dog (**like excessive barking, destructive behaviour, or changes in appetite**) is the first step to addressing this issue.

Once you've **identified** that your dog is stressed or anxious, there are several strategies you can implement.

Regular exercise, calming music, massage, and certain anxiety wraps can help. Training can also be effective in managing stress. For instance, training your dog to go to their **'safe place'** when they're feeling scared can provide them with a sense of security.

Always remember to approach these situations with **patience and understanding, reinforcing positive behaviours with praise and treats**.

## Socialization

Regular socialization is another **essential aspect** of your dog's mental health. Dogs are inherently social creatures that thrive **on interaction with other dogs and people**. Proper socialization can help **prevent behavioural issues** like aggression or fearfulness.

It's important to recall that **socialization should be a positive experience** for your dog. Always monitor their interactions to ensure they're comfortable and having fun. **Remember** the principles of positive reinforcement. **Use these principles** to make socialization a positive and enjoyable experience for your dog.

## Recognizing the Signs of a Problem

Despite your best efforts, there may come a time when you notice a change in your dog's behaviour that concerns you. It's **important** to understand that sudden behavioural changes often indicate an underlying issue—**physical or mental**.

If you notice anything unusual, don't hesitate to **seek professional help**.

Your dog's mental health is just **as important as their physical health**.

By providing mental stimulation, reducing stress and anxiety, socializing, and keeping an eye out for any problems, you can help ensure your **dog's mind stays just as healthy as their body.**

After all, a healthy dog is a happy dog—and isn't that what we all want for our furry friends?

*Photo by Linoleum Creative Collective on Unsplash*

# 8. SENIOR DOGS

One of the most rewarding journeys of dog ownership is to watch your beloved pup mature into **a calm and wise old friend**.

Senior dogs hold a special place in our hearts, **they've grown with us**, celebrated our victories, comforted us during tough times, and have taught us many life lessons about loyalty, love, and living in the moment.

But, as our dogs age, **their needs change**, and **it's our responsibility** as their trusted companions to ensure they navigate their golden years with comfort, happiness, and good health. There are different health, behavioural, and lifestyle considerations to account for, and this chapter will guide you through them.

**Just like humans**, as dogs age, they may start to encounter **health issues**.

Arthritis, vision and hearing loss, dental problems, and weight changes can all start to emerge. Their immune systems also become less effective, which may lead to **more frequent illness**.

Regular vet check-ups become even **more essential** during this phase.

We recommend **twice-yearly vet visits** for older dogs to catch any health issues early.

Don't forget to discuss **dietary changes** with your vet, as senior dogs often require different nutrients compared to their younger counterparts.

Additionally, **regular, gentle exercise is vital**. Even if your senior dog isn't as sprightly as they once were, they still need to keep moving to maintain a healthy weight and good joint health. Adapt the intensity, frequency, and type of exercise to suit their **needs and capabilities**.

In reference to our previous book, *"Puppy Training 101: A Practical Guide for Young Dog Owners,"* we discussed the significance of **mental stimulation** for dogs. For senior dogs, this remains important. Simple puzzle games, new tricks (**remember**, you can teach an old dog new tricks!), sometimes, **different walking routes** can help **keep their minds sharp**.

**Grooming is also key**, as older dogs may struggle to groom themselves as effectively.

**Regular brushing** will keep their coat in good condition and provide a good opportunity to check for any new lumps, bumps, or skin issues.

**Dental care** is important too, as dental issues can become more common in older dogs.

Finally, **love, patience, and understanding** are paramount.

Senior dogs may develop **age-related issues** like incontinence or confusion. It's essential to remember that they're not doing this on purpose – **they're simply aging**.

**Be patient**, make adaptations where needed, and **ensure they know they're loved**.

The journey with a senior dog can be an emotional one, full of its own unique challenges and rewards. **But remember, you are their world, and having your love, patience, and care means everything to them.**

Cherish the moments, embrace the challenges, and **provide the love and care your old friend deserves**.

*Photo by* **Delaney Dawson** *on Unsplash*

# SURVIVING THE FIRST YEAR: CHALLENGES, JOYS, AND THE JOURNEY AHEAD

**Stepping into the world of dog parenting,** especially with a puppy, is akin to embarking on an epic journey.

The first year is a whirlwind of **growth, transformation, trials, and triumphs**. It's a year that brings countless rewards, yet it's also filled with challenges that sometimes test your resilience.

This final chapter is here to highlight the **beauty of this journey,** providing reassurance and encouragement for the path that lies ahead.

Let's begin by **acknowledging the challenges**.

**Raising a puppy is no small task.**

The first year will **undoubtedly** be filled with sleepless nights, accidents on the carpet, and maybe even a few chewed-up shoes. Toilet training, as many of you know, requires patience and consistency. Puppies have boundless energy, and they can sometimes become overexcited and mischievous.

**However**, it's important to remember that **these challenges aren't roadblocks**, but stepping stones to a lifetime of companionship. The challenges you face are opportunities for learning, bonding, and growth, both for you and your dog.

Now, let's move on to **the joys, which far outweigh the trials**.

There's the joy of watching your puppy **explore their world** with wide-eyed wonder, their little tail wagging with excitement. The joy when they respond to their name for the first time, or when they master a command you've been teaching.

There's the sheer happiness of playtimes, the quiet comfort of snuggle times, and the **daily doses of love and companionship**.

**Remember** the first night you brought them home?

They were a tiny, perhaps slightly scared, bundle of fur. Look at them now.

They've grown, not just in size, but in personality and confidence. **They've learned to trust you, to understand you, to love you unconditionally**. And you've grown too, in patience, understanding, and empathy.

**You've become their parent, their guide, their best friend.**

As you navigate this first year, remember that **you're not alone**.

Reach out to fellow pet parents, join support groups, and **never hesitate to consult** with your vet. Refer to the advice and training techniques, the tips and insights we've shared in this book.

As we wrap up this chapter, and indeed this book, we want to remind you of one thing: the first year with your puppy is **a special, fleeting time**. Yes, it's challenging. But it's also incredibly rewarding. So **cherish** it. **Celebrate** the milestones. **Embrace** the challenges. Enjoy the journey, because this first year will lay **the foundation** for a lifetime of love and companionship with your furry friend.

**Remember**, there's no such thing as a perfect dog parent. We all make mistakes. We all have days when we question ourselves. **But every day, we try our best**. We shower our dogs with love and care. **We guide them, teach them, and grow with them**. And in doing that, we become exactly what our dogs need: we become their perfect companions.

**To all you brave, loving, resilient dog parents out there, we commend you.**

**Keep going. Keep growing.**

The journey might be long and winding, but it's also full **of love, joy, and unforgettable memories**.

Your canine companion is lucky to have you, and we're certain that you feel just as lucky to have them.

Here's to the first year, and to the many more to come!

Thank you for reading this guide on this exciting journey. Let's make it a pawsitive experience for all! Lastly, **if you found value in this guide**, please consider leaving a **review** where you purchased this book. Your feedback not only **helps us improve** but also lets other pet enthusiasts discover this resource. **Thank you** for being so supportive!

Lastly, if you found value in this guide, please consider **leaving a review on Amazon.**

Max Biscuit

https://www.maxbiscuit.com

Note from the publisher, are you into cats too?

Feline Mystique: Unlocking the Secrets of Cat Behavior and the AI Impact: Unravelling the Mysteries of Your Cat's Mind, Emotions, and Behavior from the same author.

*Photo by **Camylla Battani** on **Unsplash***

# FREQUENTLY ASKED QUESTIONS

*QUESTION: How old does my dog need to be before I start training them?*

ANSWER: You can start training your dog as soon as they join your family! Puppies can start learning simple commands as young as 8 weeks old.

*QUESTION: How much time do I need to spend training my dog each day?*

ANSWER: Aim for short, frequent training sessions each day. Ideally, try to spend 15-20 minutes per day broken up into shorter sessions.

*QUESTION: What if my dog doesn't seem to be learning?*

ANSWER: All dogs learn at different rates. Keep your training sessions fun and positive, and don't give up! Also, try to identify if there are any distractions that might be hindering their learning.

### QUESTION: Can I train an older dog?

ANSWER: Absolutely, dogs of all ages can learn new things. It might just take a bit more time and patience.

### QUESTION: Can I use the training methods in this book with any breed of dog?

ANSWER: Yes, the methods in this book are designed to work with dogs of all breeds. However, remember that each breed (and each individual dog) may have specific traits that can affect how they learn.

### QUESTION: What should I do if my dog is scared during training?

ANSWER: Never force a scared dog to perform a trick or command. Instead, try to identify what is scaring your dog and work on gradually desensitizing them to it.

### QUESTION: How can I make training more fun for my dog?

ANSWER: Keep sessions short, use lots of praise and rewards, and mix up the commands so your dog doesn't get bored. Also, try incorporating training into playtime!

### QUESTION: What if my dog only listens when I have treats?

ANSWER: Initially, treats are a great way to reward your dog for performing a command. As they get more confident, try to phase out the treats slowly and replace them with other forms of reward like praise or petting.

*QUESTION: My dog seems to forget the tricks after a few days. What can I do?*

ANSWER: Consistency is key. Practice the same tricks a few times each day and reward your dog for getting it right.

*QUESTION: Can I train more than one dog at a time?*

ANSWER: It's best to train dogs individually, especially when they're learning something new. Once they've mastered a trick, they can practice together.

*QUESTION: What's the best way to get my dog's attention during training?*

ANSWER: Use a high-pitched, excited voice to make the training seem like fun. You can also use a favorite toy or treat.

*QUESTION: My dog is doing the trick, but not on command. What should I do?*

ANSWER: Be patient and keep practicing the command with the action. They'll eventually make the connection!

*QUESTION: Should I punish my dog if they get the trick wrong?*

ANSWER: Never punish your dog during training. This can make them fearful and less likely to participate. Instead, encourage them to try again.

*QUESTION: How do I know when*

*my dog has mastered a trick?*

ANSWER: Your dog has likely mastered a trick when they can do it consistently on command in different settings.

*QUESTION: Can I create my
own tricks to teach my dog?*

ANSWER: Absolutely! If the trick is safe and enjoyable for your dog, feel free to get creative!

*QUESTION: What should I do if my
dog seems uninterested in training?*

ANSWER: Try to make the sessions more exciting with enthusiastic praise and high-value treats. You could also try a new trick to pique their interest.

*QUESTION: Can my friends
help me train my dog?*

ANSWER: Yes, it can be helpful for your dog to follow commands from different people. Just make sure everyone is using the same commands and methods.

*QUESTION: My dog seems
to be getting bored with the
same tricks. What can I do?*

ANSWER: Try introducing new tricks or incorporating the existing ones into fun games to keep them interested.

*QUESTION: Can I use the games in
the book as part of the training?*

ANSWER: Yes! The games in this book are not only fun but also a great way to reinforce the training commands.

*QUESTION: How can I tell if my*

*dog is enjoying the training?*

ANSWER: Signs that your dog is enjoying training include wagging their tail, being alert and focused, and eagerly participating in the tasks.

# BOOKS BY THIS AUTHOR

## Puppy Training 101: A Practical Guide For Young Dog Owners - New Best Buddy Dog Training Quick Guide For Kids, Teens, And Adults

Embarking on the journey of pet ownership? Welcome to the first step to turning adorable chaos into a well-behaved best friend!

Written by Max Biscuit, a passionate pet enthusiast, this quick guide delivers all the basics of puppy training in a straightforward, engaging manner, designed to appeal to readers of all ages. Whether you're a kid, a teen, or an adult, this guide will empower you with the knowledge to successfully navigate the first crucial stages of your new pet's life.

## Dog Speak: Exploring Dog-Human Dialogue And Ai's Future Role

Deciphering Dog Dialogues and the Potential of Artificial Intelligence.

Embark on an eye-opening journey into the fascinating world of dog-human dialogue with the book Dog Speak: Exploring Dog-Human Dialogue and AI's Future Role

Discover the rich history of our canine companions, dive deep into the intricate world of canine communication with this meticulously researched guide, uncovering how dogs express themselves to humans and how advancements, including AI technologies, can redefine our relationship with our four-legged companions.

## The Harmonious Household: Your Step-By-Step

## Guide To Introducing Cats And Dogs

And for families with a mixed pet household or considering introducing a new pet in their house, we have another invaluable resource. "The Harmonious Household: A Comprehensive Guide to Introducing Dogs and Cats" is a book that specifically addresses the intricacies of creating a peaceful environment for both dogs and cats to coexist.

This guide provides detailed steps on how to properly introduce dogs and cats to each other, how to interpret their behaviour, and how to solve common issues that may arise. From understanding each pet's perspective to fostering positive interactions, this book is the guide for creating a happy, harmonious home for all your pets.

## Mastering Dog Training: The Ultimate Puppy Guide For Kids, Teens, And Adults: Successfully Navigating The Exciting And Challenging First Year Of Dog Training With Your Puppy

For those who wish to dive deeper into the intricacies of dog training and pet care.

The second guide builds on the previous guide, adding advanced training techniques, extensive healthcare tips, socialization, behavioural issues, and insights on surviving the first year with a new puppy.

Together, these two books provide a complete guide for your children and the entire family, as you navigate the exciting and challenging first year of your puppy's life.

## Feline Mystique: Unlocking The Secrets Of Cat Behavior And The Ai Impact

Ever wondered why your feline friend purrs when content or chirps at the birds? Dive into the mystical world of cats and discover secrets that have eluded cat enthusiasts for years!

Why Choose This Book?
Written by the esteemed Max Biscuit, renowned for his intriguing insights into the pet realm, this book bridges the gap between traditional feline behavior understanding and the futuristic innovations of AI and technology.

Unravel the Enigma of Cat Behavior!
Decode your cat's mysterious actions, behaviors, and even those curious sounds they make. Understand why Fluffy brings you "gifts" or why Whiskers stares at nothing. With science-backed explanations, get answers to the most burning feline questions.

AI Meets Feline: A Match Made in Tech Heaven!
Explore how technology, especially Artificial Intelligence, is redefining our understanding of cats. From AI-driven toys that keep your pet engaged to groundbreaking research tools shedding light on feline genetics and behavior, this section will leave you astonished!

Inside the Book:
✓ Deep dives into feline genetics and what makes each breed unique.
✓ Tech advances, including smart litter boxes and interactive toys.
✓ The role of AI in predicting and understanding feline behavior.
✓ Tips, tricks, and advice for new and experienced cat parents alike.
Who Should Buy This Book?
Whether you're a first-time cat parent, a seasoned feline aficionado, or someone intrigued by the amalgamation of cats and AI, this book promises a purr-fect blend of science, affection, and forward-thinking insights.

Gift the joy of understanding! Perfect for birthdays, holidays, or just because you want to treat a cat lover in your life (or yourself!). Dive in now and embark on an enlightening journey into the world of cats and technology!

# ACKNOWLEDGMENT

This book is the product of a lot of hard work, dedication, and many slobbery dog kisses!  Creating this book wouldn't have been half as fun, or even possible, without our constant cheerleaders and biggest fans - our loyal golden retrievers, past and present, and our other fur-tastic pals. Their wagging tails and endless affection fuelled our imagination and gave us all the high-fives we needed. A bark out to them for being our pawsome inspiration and giving us oodles of support without asking for anything (well, maybe a belly rub or two) in return!

Lastly, if you found value in this guide, please consider **leaving a review on Amazon.**

Your feedback not only **helps us improve** but also lets other pet enthusiasts discover this resource. Thank you for being so supportive!

Max Biscuit

https://www.maxbiscuit.com

**Unlock** a world of pet care wisdom! Scan to explore Max Biscuit's top book picks, expert tips, and grab your **FREE subscription** to our exclusive newsletter.

# ABOUT THE AUTHOR

Max Biscuit, a passionate pet enthusiast inspired by the timeless bond between humans and their pets, Max Biscuit, decided to pen current knowledge, giving rise to an array of informative and insightful books that guide pet owners through every stage of their pet parenting journey. Max's guides provide practical, fun, and easy-to-understand advice, from the exuberant stages of puppyhood to the complex task of introducing cats and dogs.

Max Biscuit's ultimate goal is to strengthen the bond between pets and their human families, fostering an environment of understanding, respect, and love. And if you ask him, he'd say there's nothing more rewarding than hearing the happy tales from readers whose lives have been positively impacted by his books.

When Max isn't busy writing, he cherishes the moments spent exploring the great outdoors with his beloved dogs, engaging in playful antics with his mischievous cats, and creating nutritious homemade treats for all his pets, always on a quest for that next purr or wag of approval.

Fostering a culture of responsible pet ownership and compassion for all animals, a constant student of life, Max Biscuit embodies the spirit of a lifelong learner, constantly seeking out new knowledge about a broad spectrum of pets, from dogs and cats to rabbits and parakeets, he continues to share what is known with a singular aim: creating happier, healthier homes for pets and their human families.

**Unlock** a world of pet care wisdom! Scan to explore Max Biscuit's top book picks, expert tips, and grab your **FREE subscription** to our exclusive newsletter.